J. Newman 2017

TRANS *AM

Cis Men and Trans Women in Love

JOSEPH MCCLELLAN

ThreeL Media | Berkeley, California

Published by
ThreeL Media | Stone Bridge Press
P. O. Box 8208, Berkeley, CA 94707
www.threelmedia.com

© 2017 Joseph McClellan

All rights reserved.

No part of this book may be reproduced in any form without permission from the publisher.

Printed in the United States of America.

CONTENTS

PREFACE 7

INTRODUCTION
Outer and Inner Biographies of a Transam 19

1
NAVIGATING THE SEAS OF IDENTITY
Can We Define the Transam? 37

2
REFRAMING GENDER AND SEXUAL IDENTITIES
The Buddhist Path and the Transam 63

3
THE QUEST FOR VALIDATION
Giving Bodies Definition 89

4
WORLDS OF INTERPRETATION
How Words Hurt Bodies 105

5
AGAINST INTERPRETATION
Liberating Bodies from Restrictive Languages 131

6
THE NAKED WORLD
Merleau-Ponty's Phenomenology
of the Body without Interpretation 149

7
A PERSONAL TRANSAM SEXUALITY
My Body, My Words 165

ENDNOTES 177

WORKS CITED 194

PREFACE

For years I have wanted, and even felt a duty, to write about the topics contained in this book. I was held back by an uncertainty about what form it should take and whether I had any kind of perspective over the experiences that would inform it—namely, that at the age of twenty, in 1999, as a cisgender,[1] white, hetero[2] man, I first fell in love with a transgender[3] woman and realized the world around me saw this love as problematic. While I received understanding and support from close friends and family, there was virtually none to be found in the media or in society at large.

Over the next fifteen years, trans women would be some of my warmest friends and deepest loves. While I was aware of vibrant activism being led by trans people themselves, I found it strange that virtually no men—the friends, brothers, fathers, and especially the lovers of the trans women I knew—had anything to contribute to conversations that affected them, directly or indirectly, in so many ways. This book is essentially my extended speculative unpacking of personal experiences and observations: how I have felt in the course of loving trans women and my experiences of how they felt, how I have tried to make sense of the world that considers this love a problem, and how to speak to that world so that it may yet soften its harsh, objectifying and disempowering gaze.

From 1999 to 2013, my interest in gender studies was deeply personal, not academic. My trans friends and lovers were not scholars, so none of them turned me onto the latest writing in the field. I had some background in feminist philosophy, and it was apparent that it overlapped in many ways with the trans issues I encountered in my personal life, but I wasn't aware of the growing transfeminist literature. In 2006, in the early years of my doctorate program in Religion (Indo-Tibetan Buddhism), I read Mary Daly's radical feminist treatise *Beyond God the Father* and was taken aback by some of her transphobic comments. I was also horrified to learn, from a footnote in that book, of the existence of Janice Raymond, the archetypal anti-trans antagonist.[4] After reading her anti-transwoman screed, *The Transsexual Empire,* I discovered Sandy Stone's remarkable refutation *The Empire Strikes Back: A Posttransexual Manifesto,* which gave me my first taste of trenchant transfeminist writing.

At the time in New York City I was developing friendships and relationships in the trans community. My friend Eric Miclette, another cis hetero man who was very involved in the community, suggested I read Julia Serano's *Whipping Girl,* which planted a seed in me to tackle the subject of cis men who are attracted to trans women in a systematic way. Yet I was immersed in my doctorate program in Buddhist philosophy, and to suddenly change my dissertation proposal to transgender issues would likely have been difficult to manage. I did, however, shift my focus away from traditional Buddhist philosophy and Tibetan philology toward more immediate problems I found myself involved in. My dissertation, therefore, ended up being about the problem of Eurocentrism and institutional racism in philosophy—about the toxic social, political, and economic effects of racial (and, by extension, gender and sexual) *essentialism*. Thus my dissertation served as a testing ground for many of the arguments offered in this book. The perplexities of old philosophical texts, which I used to revel in for their own sake, mattered less and less to me if they could not be applied to my own life and the lives of my friends. An eloquent essay by the philosopher Thalia Mae Bettcher (herself a trans woman) sheds light on my own academic evolution. She writes,

> The perplexity that vexes *me,* however, wasn't revealed by the questions of some philosopher. My entire life has *already been saturated* with perplexity . . . And one of the deepest, most personal questions, it seems to me, is simply this: 'What the *fuck* is going on here?' How on earth do I *make sense* of my life as a trans★ person?[5]

I ask the same about my life as a trans*amorous* person.

When I finally had the opportunity to dedicate myself to this project, it fortuitously coincided with "The Transgender Tipping Point"[6] in popular culture, a moment of unprecedented visibility for trans people and the issues they face. Now it is not just a handful of pioneering transfeminist writers speaking out—more and more trans people are beginning to be able to express themselves with agency to ears that acknowledge their humanity. Even in the wake of this, however, we hear precious little from the lovers of trans people, especially their cis, hetero, male lovers.[7] I limit my reflections to relations between cis men and trans women because this is all I have firsthand experience of. While I have had a few trans male acquaintances and have read some of their memoirs and academic work, I do not have anything substantive to add to that discourse. While I suspect that some of this book may be relevant to trans-male transamory, I do not set out with the intention of constructing a universal transamorous theory. Rather, taking a more first-person experiential approach, I hope to encourage all kinds of transams to articulate themselves in their own way.

Moreover, I do not attempt a sweeping objective survey of the entire field of transgender studies.[8] For one thing, I am not trained for such a task, and for another, it would strike me, and I suspect others, as inappropriate for a cis man to do.[9]

Cis, white, hetero, males, after all, have historically shown a pathological need to dominate every discourse. We are the ones who have dictated the terms that have guided the ways society views trans people, and even many of the ways trans people see themselves.[10] Before anything else, we should encourage the flourishing of a trans-driven discourse, sometimes by just shutting up and allowing so many able trans voices to be audible.[11] However, I don't believe continued disinterest or disengagement is the advisable course of action for the cis-het man whose life has been tied, through love or attraction, to a trans woman. We who are cis-het men should look at ourselves and the roles we also play in a world that continues to prove unfriendly to our trans friends and lovers. Just as the interrogation of white people's place in the intersections of race and power gave rise to the salubrious field of "critical whiteness" or "whiteness studies,"[12] this book attempts something like "critical cisness."

Not being a decorated authority on transgender theory, sociology, history, or biology, I have had to supplement what I have learned in those fields with my own somewhat idiosyncratic trainings—primarily Indo-Tibetan Buddhist theory and continental philosophy. Under these influences, I dwell at length on the ethical brambles and byways that present themselves to transamorous people, the factors that affect the way we perceive those we love and desire, and the deeper metaphysical assumptions that condition our perceptions and behaviors. However, since my interest in transgender issues has never been one of academic curiosity but of deep emotional investment, the book blends theory with personal anecdotes, confessions, and speculations about failed relationships and quarrels. I hope my inclusion of these events is not purely narcissistic but of use to some readers.

I have met and heard about many transamorous men who have struggled profoundly with their attraction, falling into sexuality-centered depressions and violent behavior. Fortunately I have managed to avoid the worst of these calamities, in part due to my not being too strongly recruited at an early age into ideological positions or theoretical systems (theologies, homophobia) that would have made it more difficult for me to reconcile my attraction to trans women when it did manifest later in adolescence. A secondary benefit was that as I got older, I was drawn more and more to ways of thinking that would help me make sense of myself in relation to those I was attracted to. These included the Buddhist tradition's anti-essentialist metaphysics or worldview, and the self-sculpting techniques of Western continental philosophy. Theoretical though they may be, I believe these resources—while certainly not the only ones—are easily translated into practice and that forging more connections between them and transgender discourse can harm nothing.

Tibetan Buddhism and literature contain a prolific tradition of biography and autobiography. Biographical texts are composed and organized according to "outer," "inner," and "secret" categories. Outer biographies are rough sketches of a life, like Wikipedia entries. They tell us where a person was born and to what kind of parents; where they studied, and what subjects; who they married, where they went, and when and how they died. Inner biographies provide a glimpse into the emotional life of the subject. They are akin to the Western memoir. They talk of how they struggled with the death of a sibling at a young age, their relationships with their teachers, and the joys and sorrows that populate their lives. Secret biographies divulge the subject's deeper experience, unpacking the structures and implications of their inner life. These are something like Sartre's exhaustive plumbing of Jean Genet's mind in *Saint Genet,* or William Styron's moving analysis of his own depression in *Darkness Visible*. After a brief memoir-like introduction, most of *Transam* will resemble the "secret biography" category.

Including myself, the main subject of this book is cisgender, heterosexual, transamorous men, whether they are self-aware, incipient, or potential.[13] What is a potential transam man? It could be any man. The man who sees a pretty woman across a room at a party. He is a transam even though he squelches it as soon as someone whispers *the T*[14] into his ear. He will have to grapple with that first impression; he will always remember it. Or the man who, browsing pornography, stumbles upon the infamous "shemale" link and sees a woman as beautiful as any he's ever seen, replete with her undeniable difference. He now has a knot in his mind that may cause all kinds of sublimations. These episodes happen every day, so it is not provocative or nonconsensual to say that every hetero man is a potential transam. The object of his erotics[15] is Woman—that puzzling word that three-plus waves of feminist theory and genomic science have not been able to put their finger on. Yet, something stands in the way of the free unfolding of the amorous fire lit between this cis man and that trans woman. The chapters in this book seek to understand why this is so and ask what may be done to allow that fire to burn free of shame, anxiety, or tragedy.

I hope the book will find its way to transamorous men, as disengaged as they are, and spur them to self-inquiry and an increased intersubjectivity with their lovers. I simply want to show that transam men can and should speak up, articulate their feelings and desires, and tend to the *Mitsein*[16] that binds them relationally to their trans lovers.

Making a didactic offering to the broadest possible cis-hetero audience seems to pander to that audience, even to let them off the hook for the many years they have chosen not to use so much as a Google search to learn basic information about trans issues. The astonishingly dull and inhumane attitudes about trans people[17] and those connected to them by accident of friendship, love, or sexual attraction come often from willful ignorance—indeed, a basic delinquency of responsible citizenship, a denial of the human *Mitsein* which is everyone's birthright and duty to cultivate. Indeed, the lives of trans and transamorous people would be infinitely improved if their friends, coworkers, and especially their families understood them better. Under these circumstances, and with no wish to willfully alienate the neophyte reader, I do my best to gloss terms and not dwell too long in the philosophically arcane. But I also hope that readers will have the patience and initiative to fill in many gaps through resources easily available to them. The book's footnotes and bibliography will point them in many fruitful directions.

More than anyone, I hope the book appeals to and precipitates criticism from the demographic that inspired these speculations—trans women. In many ways this book is an attempt to repay my trans friends and lovers—to address certain frustration they always express about just what in the hell goes through the minds of transamorous men. By trying to say as much as I could about the topic after a few years of reading, reflection, conversation, and writing, I offer my pound of flesh as reparations for the abuses and obfuscations doled out by my kind, hopefully opening the door for more open communication and smoother pathways to intimacy.

While I set out with this intention, the first drafts of this manuscript bore marks of defensiveness and resentment that surprised even me. This is because, like anyone on the quest for intimacy and love, I have suffered my share of heartbreaks and humiliations vis-à-vis trans women. Therefore, I do not always write with the dispassionate voice of a philosopher, but as someone interrogating myself by asking, "What went wrong there?" "Where was this attitude or behavior coming from?" "Why did that hurt so badly?" You cannot always ask a lover who has gone for their side of the story. Sometimes I have been able to explain these to myself in terms of my own latent cissexism, misogyny, homophobia, and general benightedness and insensitivity. However, there are still some things I have not been able to concede—instances where I still believe some of my interlocutors have been either misguided or cruel.

While eliminating these commentaries might spare myself severe criticism, I believe it would be dishonest and cowardly of me to let them go entirely unheard. If nothing else, they will conveniently mark areas where cis-het men and perhaps some of their trans women lovers are not always understanding each other or communicating rationally.

Other considerations have also informed my approach. Since I began reading trans literature over the last several years, I have felt like my experience and the experiences of many of my friends and most of my lovers are not yet represented very well.[18] I have already mentioned the nonexistence of cis male writings on transamory, and while some writings by hetero trans women resonate with many and provide a valuable resource to innumerable alienated trans and transamorous men and women, there is much more to be said by people with different contexts, different values, and different histories. As I have said, none of my lovers and few of my friends have been scholars or writers, but I have learned more from them than from anywhere else.

Quite often, after an interesting conversation about our sexualities or a particular social challenge we have faced, my friends and lovers, knowing that I was an academic, have told me, "You should write about that." The general rule of thumb is to let trans people speak for themselves. However, I do not believe it is condescending or inappropriate to acknowledge that many of the people we know the best have priorities and talents outside of written social commentary and theory. It is, therefore, part of my motivation to represent many of the views of my trans female friends and lovers, both those I agree with and those I do not. Nothing in this book has been conjured from thin air; at one point or another it has been discussed quietly in a lover's arms or debated loudly in a tipsy friend's living room.

It is a foolish presumption, however, to write knowingly about what you do not know.[19] Yet just this is endlessly repeated by academics and legislators of all stripes. For generations cis "experts" have erected faulty conceptual bubbles around trans people while making almost no effort to broadcast the voices of trans people themselves. Thus, trans people have been described in the same way a group of blind men describe an elephant.[20] These experts conjure up phantom pathologies and generalized sexualities, ethologies, and therapies. It is much more chaff than grain. And the whole mess is only beginning to be cleaned up by a new generation of trans activists and writers. People new to these issues can do no better than to study Julia Serano's exquisite book *Whipping Girl,* which does not suffer the foolishness of most academic raids into trans experience. She writes,

> If sociologists truly wanted to better understand transsexuality, rather than focus exclusively on the behaviors and etiology of transsexuals, they would study the irrational animosity, fear, and disrespect that many cissexuals express toward trans people (156).

Transam attempts to do this, as well as to find ways to counter such irrational animosity, fear, and disrespect. While I inevitably opine about trans women—their motives, behaviors, etc.—based on my own experience, I know better than to pretend to analyze "the mind of the trans woman," each as different as a handprint. I try to always remind myself how this relates to me, how it *affects* me, usually in terms of how we seem to determine our own identities and sexualities vis-à-vis each other. This is generally how I answer the question I constantly ask myself: "What right do I have to talk about this?"

My connection to trans women has enriched my life in so many ways. Yet, I have seen my trans friends and lovers suffer for what seems no other reason than being trans within a hostile "cis-stem." Thus, from my unsympathetic white, cis, male perch, I have felt an imperative to interrogate myself and my demographic for ways that we fall short of giving trans people their rightful space and of allowing ourselves to live in joyful intimacy with them.

STRUCTURE

Given the lack of cis male transam memoirs, the book's introduction discusses the major events of my own personal life to provide readers with a glimpse of some of the experiences a transamorous man might go through.

In chapter one, following queer theory principles that celebrate individuality and diversity, I promote the use of the term "transam" as a non-exclusionary and even lighthearted supplementary identity label that can help organize a very large and heterogeneous population. I argue that the contemporary proliferation of identity labels is not a movement toward social chaos, but rather, by giving us resources to reject predetermined essential categories, it orients us toward a horizon where we are allowed to be and love according to our own codes. It is essential to have a neutral, light-hearted term to replace the common pejorative term "tranny chaser."

Chapter two introduces some contemporary theories of transsex and gender, highlighting the philosophical difficulty of resolving whether sex and gender are completely constructed, or if some metaphysical seat accounts for trans identities and experiences. I compare this philosophical problem with the central concern of Buddhist metaphysics: how to acknowledge and appreciate the undeniable *appearance* of a Self while at the same time not granting that Self the status of an essential metaphysical category that locks us into an anxious existential destiny.

In chapter three I analyze personal experiences and published writings to highlight the diversity of metaphysical assumptions among transgender women and cisgender men. Because these metaphysical assumptions are often so disparate, our discourse lacks a commonly acceptable starting place and pathways of communication become stuck. Since a uniform metaphysics does not seem likely any time soon, I propose that trans and transamorous discourse conscientiously move away from the ontological concepts of "real man" and "real woman" toward a more phenomenological, aesthetic description of personal experience. Phenomenological discourse not only valorizes individual experience, it can take it out of reach of the kind of metaphysical criticism based on the hostile policing of essences.

Chapter four begins by analyzing the violence and disrespect that many cis men perpetrate against trans women. I argue that the unethical treatment of trans women arises from the disruption of a mistaken epistemology that *interprets* the appearance of male and female bodies as housings for the inviolable sex and gender essences that culture uses to organize, and ultimately, misunderstand itself. I then analyze critical works from the fields of anthropology, history, and biology that support my claim that the toxic cultural climate for trans and transamorous people is fueled by an epistemology of *interpretation* that we are not, in fact, obliged to perpetuate.

In chapter five I argue that the realm of eros—when we are literally and figuratively naked—provides us with some of our best opportunities for disrupting and ultimately abandoning the epistemological habit of interpretation.

In chapter six I present the theory and method of Maurice Merleau-Ponty's phenomenological philosophy, which provides valuable resources for conceiving of and living within a world divested of gendered interpretation.

Because of society's tendency to oversexualize trans women, the discourse surrounding transamory has been mired in a self-imposed prohibition regarding the details of transamorous sexual desire. Therefore, in chapter seven, I discuss the details of my own sexuality as a way to fight against the taboos that surround the sexual aspect of transamory.

Acknowledgments

Thanks first to my parents, my brother Tyler, and my sister-in-law Jeni for their love and support, and to Kaylena Jenkins for her friendship and encouragement through the process of writing. I am also grateful to Gregory Kaplan of ThreeL Media for having faith in the project, and, together with the publishing mavens at Stone Bridge Press, for shepherding it to publication. Having written this book in more isolation than I would have preferred, I am thankful to Jodi Supanich, Yolanda Manora, and Heather Karl for editorial contributions and advice on the earliest sketches of several chapters, and to Sneha Sandez who patiently cleaned up the morass of the book's bibliography. Immense thanks are owed to Ziggy Snow who had the unenviable task of reviewing and editing the first draft of the manuscript; without their thorough and generous assistance, none of this would be fit to print.

I am thankful to friends who have, through conversations and shared experiences, directly influenced this book. On the positive side, these include Jasmine McKay, Honey Redmond, Yasmin Sim, Sonia Diaz, Bambiana Bombon, Nannisa Pitnok, Laverne Cox, Denise Medina, Pamela Santos, Nghia Nguyen, Eric Miclette, Cristy Maldonado, Nicolet Foster, Jeime Punzalan, Chris Ortiz, Jessii Lee, Dayane Calegari, Jaycee Barth, and many more. Many nameless others have influenced this book by serving out life lessons that are grist for much of its content. I am grateful more indirectly to Jason Kohn and Hanny Hindi for prodding me for many years to finally carry out this project.

INTRODUCTION

OUTER AND INNER BIOGRAPHIES OF A TRANSAM

The casual reader—the non-transam—will be curious about the nuts and bolts of a transamorous life. A few of the common questions that arise are "How did you become interested in trans women? How did you pursue that? How does dating work? Do you only date trans women? What are the mechanics of sex with a trans woman? Are you bisexual then?" Therefore, reluctantly, I offer a brief sketch of my outer and inner transam biography, which, while perhaps not very common, is not entirely unique.

Based on hundreds of conversations and observations, I believe many straight trans women have an ideal type of cis male sexual partner in mind. He is not interested in her *because* she is trans.[1] Even better if he does not even know she is trans before they meet, and for a few weeks after. He has never really even thought about trans women and certainly has never jerked off to trans porn or visited a trans sex worker. They meet by accident, in unpolluted hetero romance, perhaps at a bar, or in the supermarket, where he is none the wiser. After their love is established, they surmount the obstacle of her T rather quickly, and then they walk hand in hand into the undisturbed bliss of hetero-normative coitus;[2] he is a staunch top,[3] a real Man, an alpha male, her metaphysical, completing other-half. This is not necessarily just a fantasy. Sometimes it comes true.[4] There is no reason trans women should be excluded from having or realizing this dream; but at the same time, I believe it contains significant fairy-tale elements that are invitations to presumption and disappointment. Moreover, by representing and glorifying only narratives that conform to these wholesome parameters, we exclude a host of men and women whose attitudes and experiences are far less normative. Rather than disregarding their experiences, we should hear their stories and recognize the imperfect humanity they have in common with so many of us.

It will soon be clear that I fit none of the ideals mentioned above. I wish my own transamorous biography began more innocently, but it unfolded in an irretrievable rain of conditions and [sometimes misguided] volitions. There may be value judgments about some of my early experiences; they may threaten to impugn my basic sanity and morality and may drive some to stop reading. And the sexual details I divulge, especially in a later chapter, will surely squick[5] some people out; I have seen this firsthand when sharing drafts of these pages. Some people may simply lose respect for me the moment they learn that I reject exclusionary top/bottom paradigms; they may insist that any man who would bottom is a closet homosexual, a fraud, a fetishist, so too any man who has a preference for trans women who have not had bottom surgery. Much of this book is dedicated to interrogating where those strict attitudes come from and what their implications are. Far from exemplary, the sketches of my amorous life are as follows. . . .

*

I grew up in Denver Colorado, in upper-class suburbs during the eighties and nineties—a sea of white cis-het normativity. I was not a particularly sexual youngster. I never played "doctor" with friends, nor do I recall being an overzealous masturbator. Like most children of that era and background, when the opportunity presented itself, I would try to decipher the scrambled images of the Spice Channel—the pay-per-view soft-porn cable channel of the time—for outlines of breast and buttock. Once in while, a friend would receive the windfall of a *Penthouse* or *Playboy* from an older brother, and as we got a little older and more daring, we shoplifted them and stashed them for months or years under mattresses or in some box. Pretty boring cis-hetero fare. My crushes were always on girls.

My first exposure to a trans woman was some time in the mid or late 1980s while watching the *Phil Donohue Show*, or something like it, on a little TV in my family kitchen. As usual on those shows, the host had curated a diverse panel to shock and awe their Reagan-era audience. That day, the guest was a lovely trans woman (I wish I knew who) who submitted herself to the mob's frenzy. I don't remember any of the details—I'm sure it was the typical, "So you were born a man and you got your dick cut off?" shtick—but I remember being perplexed and annoyed that everyone seemed to think it was such a big deal and treated her with such ridicule. To me she looked lovely, like any number of video vixens I had admired on MTV. Though quite young, it was not lost on me what was different about her, but it didn't bother me at all; it even intrigued me, though I would not think of it again for many years.

My next encounter was around seventh grade. Out skateboarding in downtown Denver with friends, like the little punks we were, we snuck into the back section of a video store and flipped, slack-jawed, through the cardboard VHS displays for glimpses of the porn movies we were not allowed to rent. As luck would have it, I stumbled across a "shemale" tape (or maybe in that era's muddy nomenclature, "hermaphrodite"). There she was, a beautiful, busty woman with a penis—a visual reference point for that mysterious kind of woman I had once heard about as a little kid.[6] The experience showed me there were types of people out there we don't usually hear about, that I would probably never encounter there in suburban Denver.

Still, this visual reference didn't fuel any kind of major fantasy or sexual obsession; it was too foreign. The whole thing went way to the back of my mind and I bumbled through my teens in contact with nothing but the cis, WASP and Jewish girls I went to school with, who just did very little for me. I avoided very many amorous involvements through high school, settling for a couple of unrequited sapiosexual[7] crushes on two different school valedictorians, and the occasional one-time make-out. In the meantime, I did lot of skiing and other sports, caroused and drank with friends, and immersed myself in my idiosyncratic intellectual pursuits—literature and Buddhism—which would remain my priority for the rest of my life.

I spent the summer after eleventh grade at a Buddhist meditation center in California, where, oddly enough, I lost my virginity to a cis woman in her twenties. I was not particularly excited about her; the experience was rather disappointing. I didn't understand all the fuss. In 1997 I went to college in Seattle, and for the first two years, shyness and oversensitivity doomed me. I slept with an older waitress I had a crush on. But again, disappointment. I was too young for her. In those days I was only just learning how to use the Internet; I was a bit of a technological late bloomer. If there were dating sites, I didn't know about them. They certainly would have helped me overcome my shyness, as they did later on. Neglecting my sexual life, I read for school and studied Buddhism with my own teachers in Seattle and in California, where I spent every summer. The tradition of Buddhism I was interested in was not of the anti-sexual, monkish ilk; partnerships and sexuality were seen as part of the path, something to be thought about philosophically, not obstacles. Yet I struggled to find any romantic connections around me.

Sometime around my second year of college, I mastered the Internet for porn. There, in the cornucopia of sexual possibilities, were countless beautiful trans women. This exposure drove it home to me that trans women were indeed real, numerous, and out there somewhere. There was no fervent obsession—my young hormones still stirred to more traditional images as well—and I had very few conceptual resources for reflecting on it. It was all rather spontaneous; I just knew that a lovely trans woman pleased me aesthetically as much as anyone else did, yet there was a bit of added curiosity since I had yet to encounter a trans woman in real life and couldn't help but wonder how I would relate with her if I did. Having only a couple desultory cis-hetero sexual experiences under my belt, and seeing the different, yet still aesthetically pleasing anatomies of trans women, I imagined alternative, perhaps more fulfilling sexual and romantic possibilities. There was certainly a bit of exoticization going on—something we critical liberals generally frown upon—but it seemed an organic reaction to the Internet-age reality that was unfolding before me.

Things took a dramatic turn in my junior year, 1999, when I traveled to Brazil as an exchange student. My main motivation for going was to follow my Buddhism teacher, who had established residence there. But at the same time, a desire to explore, to meet different kinds of people, and to break out of whatever sexual shell I inhabited in my youth. I got a flight that connected through New York, where I had friends I could stay with for a few days. Unlike Denver or Seattle in the 1990s, I knew there were many trans women in New York and I wanted to meet one. But I was underage, inexperienced, and oblivious to any public venue available to me.

From the back of the *Village Voice* newspaper, I called my first sex worker, a trans woman in the West Village. I showed up, nervous as hell, wondering how being face to face would affect the attraction I had only known through computer screens. She was beautiful and I was attracted to her. She was not the warmest though; "first-timers" were clearly not her thing. Her body was surely different from the only two women I had been with before, and I wanted to test my comfort with it. I gave my first fellatio then, and tried to let her top me, which I quickly discovered I was not ready for. Afterward, I didn't feel ashamed or particularly mixed up. I felt like I had done something I needed to do; I had given myself some reference points, confirming that trans women are real, human, and knowable.

Barely twenty years old, I arrived in São Paulo and settled into my studies and a fun new social circle. A Brazilian cis woman took a shine to me, and we ended up dating for a few months. With her, finally, I learned the joys of good sex, good chemistry, and sheer pleasure. A few other Brazilian cis women showed me even more. I was no longer the demisexual[8] I had been until then; I had learned to enjoy my sexuality and even felt like making up for all the sex I had not been having through high school and college. I felt better prepared to be with a trans woman, to learn about and appreciate her body, and to give her mine—a far cry from how it felt during my clinical first encounter. Fortunately, I was in perhaps the only city with more trans women than New York, though I didn't really know what to do. This was long before OKCupid or Craigslist, and I was not familiar with the queer nightlife scene of that snarling, intimidating city. I discovered a sex work website, where dozens of Brazilian trans women advertised their services. I recognized one from a porn video I had seen the year before, and I gave her a call.

She was stunning, sweet, charming. My Portuguese had improved by then, and I could tell we were getting along extremely well. After some hours together that afternoon, she said we should hang out again, as friends. I was flattered and delighted. For the next several months I took a cab to her apartment in the city-center three, four, five times a week. We spent most of the time cuddling and making love, but it was not all about the sex. I was still inexperienced and there was nothing that exciting about what we did, though I experimented with bottoming a couple more times (I hadn't developed a taste for it). She was comfortable with her own body. She never seemed overwhelmed by dysphoria, which rubbed off on me and made me feel comfortable. I felt an intimacy I hadn't with my few previous lovers. More importantly, we went out to eat, to dance, and to movies. We talked endlessly, and my Portuguese became fluent. I loved hearing about her background, so different from my own, and I admired her for her struggles and strength. One night at a restaurant, I witnessed trans discrimination for the first time. Someone accosted her from the sidewalk as we ate and walked off. Another time, a hotel clerk was vaguely rude to her, and she said that happened all the time. I noted the way she was always cautious wherever we went, and I heard terrible stories of things that had happened to her friends.

I had never truly dated anyone consistently before. Though we avoided the terms, this was my first girlfriend, and I adored her. I was a twenty-year-old student; she was an established sex worker in her late twenties, and she continued to do her sex work when I wasn't around. I learned to compartmentalize. I didn't doubt her feelings for me, and I didn't let her work bother me very much. No doubt this formative experience influenced my accepting attitude about sex work.

I made a promise to myself that this whole thing would not be a secret; I would not be a closeted hypocrite. Having browsed enough online forums on the subject, I was aware of the tendency to fetishize trans women, and I would do my best to be self-critical. It has always been important to me to be open with my friends and to only keep friends I can be open with, so I told them about the woman I was dating, holding nothing back. When my older brother came to town to visit, I introduced him to her and we all went clubbing together. In 1999, this was a bit radical. I caught wind of plenty of gossip about me, but my best friends, after some initial befuddlement and harmless teasing, quickly processed the whole thing and moved on.

My visa was running out at the end of the year. I was only twenty. I left São Paulo to do more intensive studies in

Southern Brazil. We separated sadly but cordially. My first reciprocated love.

In southern Brazil, I immersed myself in Buddhist studies with my teacher. A young cis woman was doing the same thing. We had *exactly* the same interests and priorities. We formed a deep bond; we fell in love in our too-young, bright-eyed, idealistic state. For a variety of reasons, we never even had sex, so who knows how that would have turned out, but we connected in that mythical, spiritual way. We inspired each other and gave each other hope for a great future. We were both obsessed with our studies, and we went our separate ways to dedicate a few single-minded years to them, aspiring to meet again. The years that followed were complicated and turbulent, and our relationship never reached its romantic dénouement, but it gave me a taste of what a deep intellectual connection can feel like with a romantic partner, different from the more general comfort and affection I had with my previous girlfriend.

In 2000, I returned to Seattle for my final year of college. Brazil had made me more confident with women, but I still hated the cat-and-mouse game of cis barroom courtship, and online dating was still not really a thing. I did, however, prod myself to go to one of Seattle's big queer discos a few times. There, I found that pretty trans women would *even approach me* if I presented myself as available. I availed myself of the opportunity a few times that year, which was the extent of my sex life. I didn't date these women because, other than physical attraction and superficial affection, we just had too little in common, and not a lot to talk about. I was finishing my history degree and planning, on graduation, to move to Nepal to learn Tibetan language and intensify my Buddhist studies. I could have fun out dancing, or for a few drinks, and then to bed, but my priority was my studies.

And in 2001, at twenty-two, I went to Nepal. Almost every flight into Nepal connects through Bangkok. You can guess what I explored. Though I stayed only a couple weeks, I struck up a connection with a Thai trans sex worker, and we spent much of my time there together. It was not a particularly exciting sexual relationship to me—she was a strict bottom and did not like her genitals touched at all, which was something new to me. However, I simply felt comfortable with her and enjoyed getting to know her. Like most Thais, she was a devout Buddhist and often went to temples and made offerings to the monks. After I had already left, when I knew that my Buddhism teacher, an old Tibetan man, was traveling through Bangkok, I told her she should go visit him and tell him she's my friend. In her finest clothes, she brought him an offering and they chatted. She reported back that he was warm and welcoming, and I was glad to have made the introduction. My teacher had greatly informed my attitude about gender and sexual identity. Buddhist ethics taught me that every living being deserves compassion and respect, and Buddhist metaphysics taught me that there could be no eternal essence whatsoever, let alone the meager conditions of male and female.[9] Later on, however, I heard that this visit generated much gossip among my fellow students. While I'm confident my teacher said nothing negative, his attendants, some of whom I considered friends, were less open minded. "Why would he send some tranny hooker to meet our precious teacher?" Hearing about this saddened me, convincing me that even my Buddhist community, which had helped me open my mind so much, was blighted by regressive attitudes about sex, gender, and class.

    I am happy to say the Thai woman and I are friends to this day, keeping in touch through Facebook. She ended up marrying a Frenchman and immigrating to France. In 2010, when I was studying in Paris for the summer, we had lunch and spent a day together strolling the Boulevards.

    For two years in Nepal, I was nearly celibate. Not by choice, but because of the incredible inconvenience of trying to date in such a conservative culture, where arranged marriage is still the norm. I had one cis lover for a little while, though the relationship was much more spiritual and affectionate than sexual. We shared interests and had a bond, but her culturally conditioned sexual conservatism would inevitably have made life difficult for me. In addition I had two desultory sexual encounters with cis women there. I tried to flirt with a few others, with no success. When I left Asia, I gallivanted in Bangkok one more time—my final foray into that kind of sex work. By then I could no longer rationalize it as "educational." I knew enough; it had just become whoring. While I had benefited from the sex work industry, I wasn't comfortable becoming a habitual consumer.

When I returned from Nepal in 2003, I launched into another year of immersive studies, remaining nearly celibate in the Trinity-Shasta Mountains. While outwardly keeping up a strict discipline of practice, I wondered that year what my romantic and sexual futures had in store for me. The celibate mountain life was not promising. The choice threw disparate parts of myself into sharp relief, and I was not finished dealing with it. Wandering out of the woods to check mail one day, I found an acceptance letter to the graduate program at Columbia University in New York.

I was thrilled. Now I could study and open myself to all kinds of social and sexual possibilities. My experience was hitherto limited to some cis women lovers, only two with emotional bonds, and several trans lovers, including a few sex workers and a couple of nightclub ladies. I was still a romantic. I believed in true love, and even marriage, but I didn't know what kind of horse it would ride in on. I never wanted children, so that never factored into a cis preference. If anything, I probably preferred a trans partner although at the time I aspired to openness. My friends and brothers knew about my transamorous proclivity, and I was not afraid to tell my parents, who I am more distant from, should a serious relationship come up.

It was 2004, the golden age of Friendster and MySpace, which made it so much easier for us introverts to get dates.

The first several months in New York City were a blur. I was studying like crazy, trying to cram two years' worth of master's degree credits into one year, and still taking advantage of the city. I was not physically attracted to anyone at school, so I went on innumerable MySpace dates, very few of which I remember—mostly cis, a few trans. I also enjoyed my first Craigslist casual-encounters hookups—mostly trans, a few cis. Nothing clicked.

After several months of this kind of dating, I met a woman who rocked my world. She was eight years older than me, cis, and very glamorous with a charming accent. She worked in an art gallery and was passionate about art. When I took her out with my friends, she was funny and outgoing. After a few weeks dating, I was falling for her and we got serious. The sex was not good, no kinks, no freakiness, but not necessarily because she was cis. I would understand later that she was just not very sexual.

While my sexual experience had been growing, I was still inexperienced enough in love to think it was reconcilable, that love and affection would overcome the lack of sexual chemistry. It never did. Because of that affection, and because I decided to help her get a green card, the relationship dragged on much longer than it should have. I learned what it is to be locked into a frustrating, loving, sexless relationship. I learned it would take much more than the repetition of banal coitus to keep me turned on. Toward the end, when I expressed my sexual frustrations, my sexual openness, and my past connections with trans women, she had no way to relate and shamed me for it.

When that relationship ended, I was determined not to make the same mistake twice. More dating, I took care not to fall for a heteronormative, vanilla,[10] cis woman so quickly again. I visited a dominatrix for the first time and got in touch with my kinky side, connecting to a circle of dominatrix friends with whom I formed close bonds. I started to find relaxation and satisfaction in bottoming, and I learned it was something I could do just as easily with cis women. It felt good to subvert the heteronormative roles that had always either bored me or given me anxiety. I focused a bit more on trying to date trans women, but kept running into that same lack of common interests. More than a few times, the script was flipped. I was rejected, too. At least one trans lover laughed at me when I suggested our possibly dating.

I ventured into the infamous "tranny parties" in the city, mostly full of working girls, but where friendships are not impossible to find. I ended up becoming very close, platonic friends with a prominent trans party promoter from that community; we were roommates in Midtown for a year. We were like brother and sister. I helped her with parties she promoted, working as a doorman. I was accepted into the community. Women became comfortable being my friend; many of those friendships would endure. With some relief, I felt I had shaken the "chaser"[11] label, at least in the eyes of those who took the time to get to know me.

Also, while working the door, I got to meet and talk to hundreds of other transamorous men from all walks of life. The vast majority came alone and uncomfortable, standing near the wall hoping to pick a woman up for a few hours. Many were married and out for a night of spice before returning to their cis female partners. A strange older man we called "Mr. Burns"[12] used to come in with a scarf wrapped around his head and lurk nervously until he could negotiate with someone to leave with him as soon as possible. Rumor had it he was a high-level judge. There were college boys, white-collar guys, blue-collar men from the outer boroughs, bisexual men who would sometimes hit on me, and hypermasculine security guards who might hook up on the sly with the women attending the party. Every week a good dozen of these men would hover around me while out for a cigarette, chatting with me about the women there and how they related to them. Very few dated the women openly; the vast majority revealed to me just how far society is from perceiving trans women in a humane and healthy way. "Some of these girls are hotter than *real* girls!" they would say with a smirk, eliciting awkward pseudo-philosophical defensiveness from me. Some would tell me about the problems awaiting them at home for "coming out" with these women. There was always an issue when some man feared himself captured in the background of a selfie and would beg or threaten until the pic was deleted. Since cis men don't write about their relationships with trans women, I learned a lot at that job from listening to so many conflicted men open up a bit to me about their transamory. Before then my only source of information were the horror stories my trans friends and lovers told me about their experiences, but I never got to hear anything from the men themselves.

One of my roommate's good friends was a well-known trans porn star. She lived out of town but visited often. After my lengthy relationship with a cis "good girl" that made me question the viability of my own sexuality, she was just my type and I asked her out. We got along like peas and carrots. She was funny, bright, sweet, and had a fascinating biography. And the sex . . . oh my. She was experienced and sexually confident, dominant, kinky. I fell in love with her and we dated solidly for a year. She came to every dinner party and BBQ my friends invited me to, hung out with my brother and his girlfriend when they visited, and we spent the holidays together. I know they enjoyed some gossip and jokes at our expense, and I prompted lots of conversation, but after getting to know her, they all became cis-trans ambassadors. This woman and I were in love and highly sexually attracted to one another, but there was not enough common ground for us to share to make it last longer.

In a heavy-hearted cloud beneath the ruins of that relationship, I holed up and drank. Then a friend invited me to his friend's art event. When I met her, I knew I was in for it. It felt too soon to be dating again, but I was like a moth to her flame.

This talented, creative, passionate, spiritual trans woman read a lot and wrote beautifully. We talked about literature and music—her taste was impeccable (and so like mine!). She was cool but down-to-earth, funny and edgy. Every friend who met her looked at me, as if to say, "You finally found her." I thought *this is the person I could truly love*.

I was infatuated and determined not treat our relationship lightly. But fate was cruel. Shortly after meeting, her career was taking off; she had to leave abruptly and terminated contact with me. When she came back to New York, there was a brief rekindling, but then she disappeared again without explanation. I was shattered; and never really got over it.

Gradually, I pieced together that one of the reasons I was rejected was because of my sexuality—I was not a pure top. This realization had a traumatic impact that would influence my sexuality. For a long time there was shame and self-loathing for not living up to what was expected of me, which later turned to bitterness and a self-protective repulsion from all strict bottoms (trans *or* cis) looking for me to be a pure top. I was happy to top when I was genuinely attracted to a new person after a date or two, but as soon as I got the feeling that our entire sexual-romantic edifice rested on the foundation of my erection, I felt the impending awkwardness and embarrassment of having to tell them that I cannot subsist on coitus, and I lost interest. Regretfully, sometimes I disappeared. As someone who is not naturally alpha or dominant, cajoling or teaching a sexually inexperienced person does not come easily, nor am I attracted to the proposition to "just take what you want," as some submissive women have exhorted. As I mature, I try to learn about a potential partner's desires and boundaries before getting involved sexually, and, when appropriate,[13] communicate my desires to them.

I dated rarely in the years that followed. Sometimes I would make a new friend, trans or cis, who was attractive and with whom I had a strong connection in some ways. In the past, I likely would have asked if they wanted to date; now I was wary and quick to throw up boundaries. Apprehending a likely sexual incompatibility, or some subtler obstacle, I valued lasting friendships more than tenuous romances that might undermine those friendships. I compartmentalized—my good friends here, casual hookups there.

I met and dated a beautiful cis woman, who was a hilarious and had a huge personality. We began as friends, and I opened up to her about my heartbreak. To my surprise, she started having feelings for me, but I was skeptical about our compatibility. As I got to know she was bisexual, kinky, quirky, and sharp as a whip, we started dating. We were open and a bit wild. She wasn't afraid to top me. Her outsized personality led the way, and we were tight. People in my life said they had never seen me happier; we were yin and yang.

We dated for four years. It was not always easy; we could clash, but it looked like it might be that imperfect partnership that lasts a lifetime. Then, we both hit a hard year, stressing over our careers and finances. I was finishing my PhD and had no job prospects for the next year. Her frustration grew and openness waned. She started to want a more normal life, including a more normal sex life. Heteronormative coitus became our dispiriting staple. Again, I felt shamed for not being a pure top, for not being more of an alpha male. Our sex life crumbled.[14] It ended in frustration and bitterness on both sides, and I resolved from then on to communicate very clearly with future romantic partners that I am not just versatile but in fact mostly bottom. Take it or leave it. While I still believe the right person could inspire me to return to topping (since I have managed to live happily for years being topped only once every few months), I never want to put myself in the position to be shamed and abandoned for that reason again.

Since then, I have had cis and trans lovers, mixing some bad luck and some bad choices. Pursuing an academic career forced me to move a lot, sometimes just as I'd met someone I was really interested in. At present I live in Chittagong, Bangladesh, and I do not have access to any sexual subcultures where I might meet (other than by chance) partners who do not subscribe to strict gender roles. Therefore, in practice, I am celibate, except when I am able to travel occasionally to Kolkata, Bangkok or other large cities where like-minded partners are easier to find. I am careful not to date any seriously vanilla types, cis or trans—anyone with dogmatic attitudes about heteronormative top/bottom sexual roles. I dislike enacting hyperbolized dominant or daddy personas that can hypostatize sex and gender paradigms; my thoughts on this distaste recur in the following pages. While not enthusiastically polyamorous, I have little faith in the tenability of strict monogamy. I have learned that it is worth it to communicate all of these things up front with potential partners, which leads to one of the most serious ethical conundrums of transamory—when and to whom does one broach the topic of sexual desire and preference?

Because of the disproportionate exploitation of trans women by the pornography industry, labor discrimination that drives a disproportionate amount number into sex work, combined with the media's constant portrayal of them as sex workers and deviants, trans women are overly sexualized in the popular imagination.[15] When this imaginary of the hyper-sexualized trans woman spills over into the dating world, it can be particularly frustrating and even infuriating. Many trans women have noted how, especially on social media and dating apps, the conversation tends to skip the part where you ask the person questions about their job and background, very often turning quickly to genitalia and sexual fantasy.[16]

Such a breach of common courtesy is unforgivable. But how does a person get an idea of a prospective partner's expectations without being objectifying? Of the online dating sites, OkCupid has survey questions that offer a chance to disclose your preferences in a slightly discreet way. I have answered as many survey questions as I could, and I include a short line on my main page, requesting people to look into them before contacting me. I would prefer that my date know that I do not identify as dominant, and that I prefer nonnormative types of sex. It is sad to go on a date with someone you are physically attracted to, and indeed even like, only to find out after a few dates that your kinks, or perhaps the entire framework in which you place gender and sexuality, are impossible to reconcile. Just as the vast majority of women who might be interested in me assume from my appearance that I am all top, I infer, based on twenty plus years of dating experience, that the feminine women I am attracted to are all bottom, unless they give me some hint to the contrary.

There are few other sites that facilitate relationships between non-top men and non-bottom women.[17] Gay hookup apps such as Grindr and Scruff have opened themselves to trans users, but those highly sexualized ecosystems often encourage extremes of frankness or coyness. I have met some lovely women on those apps with a profile that tries to express my openness while still being upfront about my vers or vers-btm predispositions.[18] Disappointment has occurred many times when both parties just rolled the dice and hoped to find what they liked without ever communicating it. I'm not saying it is rational, but in the past I have met people I was attracted to and enjoyed their company. But perhaps a little bottom-shaming[19] incident was still fresh on my mind, and I didn't want to put myself in that kind of situation again, so the date fizzled out. We were both projecting onto each other, and I could not envision breaking the deadlock. Of course, sometimes there are surprising pleasures with casual sex. But chat rooms and barrooms are not ideal venues to find a date. In the meantime, I will continue not to ask about people's genitals or sexual preferences, but I also pine for the day we are not shaming each other.

NAVIGATING THE SEAS OF IDENTITY
CAN WE DEFINE THE TRANSAM?

Based on conversations with friends and acquaintances, and reading online discussions, published essays and memoirs,[1] I believe a large number of trans women resent and continue to reject any effort to validate cis—especially, but not exclusively, male—attraction.[2] They may be distrustful of, even disgusted by a cis person, perhaps especially a cis man, who would expressly consider trans identity to be an attribute of special attraction—that is, who could self-identify as transamorous. They assume that to name this affinity is objectifying and Othering. Some friends advise me that the term transamorous once again trans people, especially women, into the object of a fetish; it's just another, anodyne name for the rightly despised "chaser."[3] To identify with trans-oriented attraction therefore seems misguided and irresponsible at best, reprehensible and dangerous at worst. This seems to me to lead us to an impasse. If the transamorous person is constrained from naming their love, their individuality is denied and they are compelled to dissimulate or sublimate their attraction. The trans lover suffers from this arrangement too; their "transness" is tagged with an unnecessary metaphysical heaviness that also must be dissimulated or sublimated. In place of the common pejorative term "chaser," a welcoming but accurate term can help resolve this conundrum.

Due to actual and historical relations of power, the cis man's attraction to a trans woman is arguably the more problematic situation, whereas the cis woman's attraction to a trans man is complicated in other, less obvious ways.[4] And for some (not all) trans women, it may seem that in order to mirror (or complete?) her identity, her ideal partner would be a straight man. To be fair, after eons of investment in their dominating identities, cis men have fully earned the distrust of their intentions with trans women. Cis men have largely devised and profited from the gendered economy of external validation in which the "Real Man" is the referential gold standard that sets terms for the "Real Woman," and so many other fabricated metaphysical terms to label those who are Other, or less, than the "Really Real" (White) Man. While raking in the rewards of this economy, cis men are expected to be consistent, at least, and repose in our unassailable Manhood—a simple truth about reality—and imagine anything Other to be something with a significance relative only to their own.

More often than not, however, I think the objections to the transamorous identity of a cis man are based on an idealization. If we pronounce "Woman" and "Man" with enough conviction, through sheer power of will we can homogenize the differences between us; there will be no need to identify as trans at all. Even "male" and "female" could become two sides of a single coin (in "holy matrimony"), and all individuality and diversity can be dissolved once and for all. I lack confidence in metaphysical assumptions that fuel this faith, and I believe most of the terms that would sustain an abstract discourse about Man and Woman are, and could only ever be, borrowed from the cis-het patriarchy, an oppressive global superstructure in which cisgendered, heterosexual men hold a disproportionate access to power.

Condemning cis men who wish to articulate a distinct sexual attraction to trans women seems to avoid, deny, or suppress a real phenomenon that is not, to my mind, invalid—however problematic it may truly be in our present context. There are, and will continue to be, people who consider "trans" identity to be an attractor in a sexual partner.[5] My own attraction to trans women has been evident to me for nearly twenty years and has remained largely unchanged after withstanding much critical scrutiny. I will not be ashamed of my desires, and I am not convinced they are a species of pathology. Moreover, putting my own defensiveness aside, the hasty conflation of any transamorous man with the disapproved "chaser" could have the effect of shaming and silencing transamorous people whose affinity is even far less pronounced than my own.

Take, for example, the hypothetically ideal straight cis male partner for a trans woman. He did not know his partner was trans at first, or maybe had never dated a trans woman before, so her trans identity played no role in his attraction to her. They have a rich and loving relationship for some months or years, and then the relationship fails for some common, predictable reason. This man now has a bank of memories about his former partner. He may recall how one of the things that made him fall for her in the early stages of the relationship was that he found her trans biography interesting and admired her for her life experiences; he found it enriching, under her influence, to learn more about his social environment. It became important for him to interrogate his cis privilege; he clicked with her friends and had eagerly taken part in some trans activism with them. He may also recall intimate moments, her body and the ways they made love, which presented him with a new understanding of his own gender and sexuality.

Now, of course, all of this experience occurred because she is a woman, full stop. However, according to the prevailing discourse, once the relationship with this particular woman who is trans comes to an end, the man must exorcise all of those positive associations that had to do with his former partner's *trans*gender or sexual identity. If he now seeks another trans partner as a way of again touching upon those fond feelings, he has slipped into pathological fetishization.[6] The only thing that could both satisfy this new affinity in him and save him from accusations of being a fetishist would be if he happened again to stumble upon a trans woman unawares. The likelihood of this accidental occurrence recurring after he has already been involved with a trans woman, her friends, and her community is, however, somewhere between low and nil.

In a magnificent PhD dissertation[7] and follow up essay,[8] Avery Tompkins analyzes this conundrum among the cis female partners of trans men. Their dilemma is not entirely different from that of straight cis transamorous men. Reflecting on her subjects' video testimonials about their relationships, Tompkins writes:

> In her vlog, Beth notes that a failure of available terms to describe her attractions positively means that if she tells someone she is attracted primarily to trans guys, she is labeled a "tranny chaser." Lacking language to adequately describe her attractions and sexuality, and knowing the danger around speaking these attractions at all, has led Beth to simply not identify with any sexual identity label. So, while there is certainly a potential impact on the trans partner in a relationship who may not have their trans identity affirmed, the cis partner in that relationship is also unable to discuss their own sexual identity in relation to "trans" (Tompkins, 2014: 772).

And relating to my previous consideration of our hypothetical male's erotic memories of his trans partner, Tompkins observes that their[9] subjects "seem to be engaging in a careful and explicit denial of the erotics of transness in order to resist classification as a 'tranny chaser'" (773). Tompkins contends "that the silencing of 'trans' as desirable or erotic does not align with a sex-positive politics" (774) inasmuch as their subjects "were specifically denying any kind of attraction to the trans-specificity of their partners, preferring to say something akin to: "I just like him for him" instead of reveling in (or even bragging about) the erotics of their partner's transness as some have begun to do in other contexts."

My experiences suggest there is a common imperative to deny an attraction to certain *trans* qualities, whether history or physiology, of a trans partner. There are quite a few published discussions of the "tranny chaser" phenomenon, which express different attitudes about the possibility of a non-pernicious trans affinity.

Christin Milloy has put the matter in all fairness:

> When a cis person is attracted to a trans person, that should never be viewed (in and of itself) as a fetish, because that would cast any relationships between trans and cis people as shameful . . . But what about when cis people specifically seek out sex with trans bodies, in a way that serially objectifies us, and disrespectfully treats us as their kink? . . . While their attraction for trans people mustn't be stigmatized, their bad behavior toward trans people absolutely should be. . . .[10]

As someone who accepts his position in the crosshairs of such a critique, I find nothing at all to object to there.

From another angle, Charley Reid focuses on what she perceives as a tendency for transamorous men to reduce a trans woman to her physical features, taking no interest in her character or biography. Reid writes:

> As trans women, how are we supposed to be with someone who has stated that their reason for being attracted to us has nothing to do with our personality or our tastes or our perspective on life, but with our particular configuration of body parts? Moreover, how are we supposed to feel when our culture

assumes this kind of sexualization is the only way for us to be wanted?[11]

When I read this passage from my own perspective as a self-identified transamorous man, it horrifies me to know there would be people who know and say they are attracted *only* to the physical features of a trans woman. I emphasize "only" because, as Tompkins suggests, we can distinguish between those who see trans identity as one characteristic among many others, and those who might consider trans identity to mean *only* a physical attribute. It is upsetting for me to hear that some men do confuse genuine mutual attraction with a passing interest in bodies.[12] I agree such men are not recognizing trans women, but it does not lead me to conclude that no man can ever have a sexual or romantic preference for trans women, among other preferences.

Undoubtedly, as Reid's point appropriately implies, the history of exploitation and dehumanization of trans women in particular makes the ethics of transamory particularly problematic. The particularities of the identity "trans woman" merit the extensive consideration I give in these chapters because a self-identified transamorous man presupposes her particular identity. Having a fetish can be an issue between sexual partners, but I assume, in principle, society can tolerate all kinds of diverse sexual activities between *consenting adults* and not explode. To be sure, transamory is particularly problematic for historical reasons. Yet there are plenty of cases where a person is desired for their height, their breasts or penis size, their accent, or any number of attributes marked as uncommon or fetishistic objectifications, and exploitation or dehumanization does not necessarily follow as a consequence. My point here is not to establish an equivalency between these or any objects of fetishization (for, there are some that most certainly push boundaries of what constitutes consent or harm), but to draw the most relevant ethical distinction. The distinction, I believe, assumes the ethical weight is not derived from the objectified body (its configuration, for example), but from the objectifying behavior and its ethical implications. When any of these forms of making a fetish of a feature becomes a pattern, when the person with this "preference" seems to *privilege* this one attribute over many other considerations of the person's full range of features, they open themselves up to ethical criticism.[13] The reduction of an infinite subjectivity's fullness to a finite object's narrowly delineated feature(s) merits ethical criticism. The objective attributes—which arguably do *not* define the subject—are, it would seem to me, neutral per se to ethical judgment; that is, an objective attribute, even more specifically a physical feature (like configuration), is objectified in some contexts differently than in others, under some conditions but not others. The problem is not this or that attribute as such, be it trans feminine or something else. The problem is that we face essentialism or objectification as an act, and though I certainly acknowledge that trans women are particularly vulnerable to this reduction for unfortunate—and hopefully rectifiable—historical and cultural reasons, nonetheless I contend there is no moral or ontological reason to distrust trans attracted identities any more than lovers of skin ink or large feet.

    I do not consider myself a serial dater, so often a year or two has passed before I have felt a strong enough connection with someone to date them seriously. In the interim, the preponderance of my casual lovers has tended to be trans women largely owing to the resources of Craigslist, Grindr, and Scruff. Upon serious self-reflection, I will honestly say that I have never dated a trans woman *only because* she was trans. Humor, intelligence, political views, and character have always taken precedence for me above all physical attributes. If I were considering pursuing two women who both had an array of qualities I found attractive, and one of them was a trans woman, I would admittedly factor it in as an attribute that might tip the scale her way, but it would not be such an important factor that it would outweigh many other considerations about her personality and values.

Although I recognize my privilege as a cis man (a position I would like to approach with the utmost humility) I am not entirely content to concede the entire discourse of trans affinity to trans identified people because the discourse is occasionally referencing and judging *my* identity. And while I take in trans people's perspectives, opinions, and arguments, they do not always accurately describe the nuances of *my* own experience. I want to hear trans identified people speak; but I would like to speak too. My debt to Avery Tompkins' work on trans men and cis women is large. Of trans affinity, they write:

> These discussions cannot be held without cis people. While I recognize the value in trans-only conversations and spaces, denying cis people the ability to take part in conversations around transsexualities seems detrimental to a sustainable sex-positive trans politics, especially if there are arguments circulating that cis people are doing the majority of the fetishizing or "tranny chasing." Cis people are not inherently incapable of taking part in sex-positive and affirming discourse about trans identities and bodies, but they are certainly the individuals most at risk for being labeled "tranny chasers," which may limit what cis partners and allies believe they can say about their attractions and desires. (2014: 775)

We have already seen the subjects of Tompkins' study struggle to find suitable words to describe their relationships with trans partners. A compulsory silence limits the range of their amorous experiences to the drabbest shades of grey, cramming diversity into readymade hetero- or homo-normative binary categories. "Who tops and who bottoms?" is not a relevant question for understanding cis-trans (or any?) sexual relations.

More precise language is necessary, and the fears of increased articulacy, in the face of magnifying potential offense, need to be assuaged.

This need for precision is evident when we examine the more hostile criticisms of transamorous people, such as we find in Princess Harmony's 2016 article for *The Establishment*. Here Harmony categorically prohibits the use of any term that might mark an affinity for trans people. She writes, "Even the phrase itself—'trans-attracted'—demonstrates how this fetish is inherently transmisogynistic. If those who identify with this label saw trans women as real women, they wouldn't need a word to differentiate us from other women in order to explain their attraction to us." This statement wades deeply into contested territory. I believe, and I will argue throughout, that using the language of "real women" is more harmful than a term like "trans-attracted." The former encourages us to think of Woman or Womanhood as a fixed metaphysical essence, which is something feminist and transfeminist theory,[14] and even social and medical science,[15] has been chipping away at for a long time. Moreover, the linguistic marking of trans is something that is part of the everyday language of trans people themselves, as well as their friends and partners. Where is a trans or queer community in which distinctions between cis and trans are not made every day, in many contexts? If marking a person as cis or trans is seen as commonplace and harmless in certain social contexts, a more thorough analysis is required to show why it must be forbidden in all romantic or sexual contexts. In the same article, Harmony goes on to paint a very dark picture of cis male "allies," implying that the majority of them are just fetishizers who have learned a new way to exploit trans women sexually:

> Trans fetishizers often perform love on multiple levels. At an individual level, they befriend or romance us, feigning care and affection. On a societal level, they partake in ally theater in order to create the illusion

that they care about us as people and our rights as a whole. But their love can quickly turn into hate—especially if we turn down their sexual advances ... I've known far too many trans women who have been violently harmed by "trans-amorous" men to believe that they are capable and dependable allies.

This passage makes a leap. Regrettably, men generally have a tendency to act this way. For example male professors acting as caring advisors to female students can exhibit similar behavior,[16] and we are all too familiar with the predations of religious leaders. Recently, some friends of mine uncovered a scandal in Kolkata's spoken-word poetry scene where a well-known male organizer in that community was exposed as a serial harasser.[17] Similar cases have been documented in social activist movements.[18] Criticizing individual harassers is imperative, as is recognizing patterns of abuse and exploitation, but these can be done without suggesting that every, or at least most men with a particular preference, are motivated by predatory impulses. Harmony pursues a line of reasoning that is not entirely unsubstantiated but results in a number of cynical entailments that seem intent on limiting cis ally-ship rather than critically distinguishing its varieties.

Harmony writes:

> The trend of playing the role of an ally to gain access to certain populations is by no means, sadly, unique to the trans community. The phenomenon also plays out, for example, among men who have fetishes for women of color and learn about anti-racism, while secretly continuing to be racist and harboring race play fantasies. I know other women of color who have had their hearts broken by fetishizers who treated them as sexual objects based on their race without ever truly loving them.

The description of certain realities is fair enough. And I can't help but be reminded here of the times I have gone on dates with self-proclaimed "sapiosexuals" whom I came to discover—as they mischievously confessed, "I've always wanted to sleep with a professor"—[19] could not have cared less about *my* thoughts or work or much at all about me for that matter. The cruel misdeeds of these types of fetishizers are thoroughly trounced in Harmony's piece, but there is no distinction made between them and allies, leaving the reader with the impression that no cis man could ever be a true ally to trans women. This would be a surprising conclusion, and I could imagine that was not the final intention of the author, yet to my eye, it is how the text reads.

Harmony concludes:

> Fetishizers posing as allies use all the buzzwords. They speak on panels about "loving" trans women and supporting the trans community. They do everything they think an ally is supposed to do, but it's all rooted in problematic sexual goals. Some of these speakers and supposed activists have been known to harm or fetishize trans women, but because they learn the language of social justice, this aspect of their behavior and the violence behind it tends to be overlooked—except of course, by us. But we know that too often, our "allies" are harboring ulterior motives. Learning about the intricacies of societal oppression solely for the purpose of gaining sexual access to people is a wicked type of violence ... What good is gathering allies who replicate the harm that we are organizing against? Nothing positive can be achieved by teaming up with people who—subconsciously or not—objectify and other us.

This is an aggressively cynical line of reasoning, which seems to universalize a particular case and uses the false will of some (perhaps many) perpetrators to render pathological a preference or predilection. Any cis lover of a trans woman or ally to trans women is de facto a predator. While not cited, I would assume that Harmony has in mind a well-documented incident in 2016 in which the Chicago activist group Creating Change hosted a panel for trans-attracted men to talk about their experiences.[20] A group of young trans women disrupted and shut down the panel, bringing to light that one of the main participants in the panel had a problematic history of abusive relationships with trans women. From what I have been able to learn about this incident, it seems to me that the protesters rightfully exposed an instance of egregious hypocrisy.[21] The risk in making universal assertions based on a particular case, however, is that it vilifies *every* potential ally, painting them as wolves in sheep's clothing. Having a suspicious or skeptical attitude seems to me a different claim than the passage above makes. According to the argument put forth by Harmony, it would appear that all of my platonic trans friendships are a cover for my sexual predation, and the thousands of hours I put into researching and writing this book are bricks in the road toward increased access to trans communities where I can live out my exploitative fantasies.

I do not think Harmony's suspicions are wild or without grounds; however, I do believe the conclusions she reaches too extreme. For example, when I first moved to the San Francisco Bay Area, my closest contacts were platonic friends who are trans women, both of whom I had known for many years. Knowing both of them were involved in San Francisco's rich trans networks, it would be disingenuous of me to hide that the thought crossed my mind, "I wonder if they have any friends I might click with." I was thinking along the lines of looking for a serious relationship. The same thought crosses my mind when I start a new job. "How nice it would be if I met someone I click with in this new academic scene." It has always seemed to me a bad idea to sleep around within your own circle of friends and acquaintances. When I am introduced to friends of friends I am attracted to, I tend to be *very* cautious about going down the path of flirtation so as to avoid the social awkwardness that ensues after a failed romance with a friend of a friend. In the Bay Area, my friends introduced me to dozens of other trans women, several of whom I was attracted to physically, but there were never enough complementary factors like shared interests that ever justified my dating within those circles. In fact, I felt largely unwelcome as a cis white man. By the end of my year there, I had stopped trying to fit in to the paradoxically uniform queer scene, and mostly spent time with my original two friends in more one-on-one settings, where our friendship looked exactly like anybody else's close friendships. It would take a lot of convincing to get me to agree that my years-long relationship with these friends was based on a hope of sexual opportunities they might cast my way.

*

It is helpful to keep in mind that in queer culture *t4t*[22] is seldom darkened by the same shroud of pathology. Trans people, after all, did not invent the system that has been so hostile to them for so long; they are entitled to appreciate each other, to name and celebrate their remarkable nuances, to build communities, and to find partners who understand and empathize with their experiences. To understand what is happening here, I turn to Julia Serano, a trans woman who happens to be attracted to other trans women—and *especially* trans women. Although I do not have the perspective Serano does, and I do not wish to appropriate her writings about trans identity to support my own phenomenological account, I readily acknowledge I have learned a tremendous amount from how she frames a trans person's own transamory.

Serano gives an eloquent reply to her interlocutor's

question, "So if it's not about genitals, what is it about trans women's bodies that you find so attractive?"

> I paused for a second to consider the question. Then I replied that it is almost always their eyes. When I look into them, I see both endless strength and inconsolable sadness. I see someone who has overcome humiliation and abuses that would flatten the average person. I see a woman who was made to feel shame for her desires and yet had the courage to pursue them anyway. I see a woman who was forced against her will into boyhood, who held on to a dream that everybody in her life desperately tried to beat out of her, who refused to listen to the endless stream of people who told her that who she was and what she wanted was impossible.
>
> When I look into trans women's eyes, I see a profound appreciation for how fucking empowering it can be to be female, an appreciation that seems lost on many cissexual women who sadly take their female identities and anatomies for granted, or who perpetually seem to cast themselves as victims rather than instigators. In trans women's eyes, I see a wisdom that can only comes from having to fight for your right to be recognized as female, a raw strength that only comes from unabashedly asserting your right to be feminine in an inhospitable world. In a trans woman's eyes, I see someone who understands that, in a culture that's seemingly fueled on male homophobic hysteria, choosing to be female and openly expressing one's femininity is not a sign of frivolousness, weakness, or passivity, it is a fucking badge of courage (Serano 2007: 279-80).

I hope not too many would criticize Serano's paean for being fetishizing or patronizing. In giving my own phenomenological account, I cannot deny that I have felt similarly in the presence of trans women lovers.[23] In my first romantic relationship with a trans woman when I was twenty, I would offer less articulate, but similar answers to the same question, like "I think she's badass for being who she wants to be in spite of so many obstacles." When I took in what my girlfriend had experienced in life, I felt enormous respect. More than almost anyone I'd known, she was her own person, true to herself. Her pride was not motivated by resentment. I admire this kind of high self-regard in the face of antagonism in anyone when I see it. It is perhaps the same reason some of us seek friendship or romantic partnership with artists, activists, anarchists, or nonconformists. Although, admittedly, transamory has a distinctive flavor because it concentrates charged issues around gender and sexual identity—in addition, often, to race, class, politics, aesthetics, and ethics.

To be sure, there is a fine line between respecting and idealizing or romanticizing. A trans friend has told me how annoying it was when her college classmates, albeit with the best of intentions, often looked into her eyes to tell her earnestly, "You are so brave!" She was the only trans person her classmates had ever met, and she obviously made a good impression on them, but it's easy to see how patronizing it could sound to come from a cis person praising a person because of a presumed essential quality. When we are close friends with someone we respect or admire, even if their emotional fortitude or life experience played a role in why we were first drawn to them, we do no constantly think about, let alone remind them, that we think they are brave. That admiration is simply subsumed into the growing layers of affection and attachment. No person transitions in order to be a hero, let alone superhuman. The faults of idealization do not however, I argue, preclude the genuine feeling and expression of admiration.

At twenty years old, I had some vague intuitions about why I was drawn to trans women, but not a lot of wider perspective. One of the first times I realized there was probably much more to say about it was around 2008 when I read Jean-Paul Sartre's book *Saint Genet*. I recall how, reading it on the beach next to my trans girlfriend with whom the sexual novelty had long dissipated, I felt like Sartre's admiration of Jean Genet had parallels to my own of trans people. In no way am I comparing trans people to Jean Genet, who was known just as much for his unabashed, inveterate sexual deviance as his writing. The details of Genet's sexuality have little to do with the comparison. Sartre admired Genet precisely because he was the most radical practitioner of existentialism he had met, all the more since Genet could not care less about the labels.

In Sartre's existentialism, a subject finds himself or herself subjected to the world, *thrown* into it,[24] for no apparent reason. The arbitrariness, indeed the absurdity, of our human situation inexorably produces anxieties and malaise. The subject's duty, or only hope of ameliorating this pain, is to accept it, establish some kind of agency, and sculpt his or her life according self-identified values. We cannot do anything about the real conditions that circumscribe our finite lives. Yet despite the objective finitude of our living in the world, there remains remarkably an endless horizon of possibility open to us within those limits (beginning with interpretation and ending, perhaps, with transformation). One free choice we all have is to accept the finite conditions, or not. Moreover, many limitations of our situation appear or seem real but are, in actuality, fabricated or mythological. We can differentiate the world we are thrown into from the self we aspire to become; we are thrown into a world that is projected before us. Consequently, we might grasp onto small shards of agency and make interventions; and whoever weaves those shreds into a meaningful, or beautiful, life could well be admired.[25]

As Genet wove the random fragments of his world into a kind of beautiful life, he did not curate and revel in his queerness or relish his clashes with the prevailing norms,[26] and yet he refused to hate himself for not fitting in either. Genet accepted being thrown arbitrarily into a situation (the world) and, in equal proportion, valued his own organic being; he did not seek to become a coherent system hammered together or taken apart through reason or analysis.[27] In a parallel manner, many trans people seem, through their journey of transition,[28] to step over or, at least, face squarely the trap of identity that Sartre describes.

> We ascribe more reality to what others teach us than to what we could learn by our self. Out of submission or respect, we take information which, in any event, is only probable as being an unconditioned certainty. On the other hand, we are tempted to regard the information of our unconsciousness as dubious and obscure. This means that we have given primacy to the object which we are to Others over the subject we are to our self (33).

The trans people whom I have known best and admired most have, in my experience of them, discovered for themselves that they are not a broken being whose ruptured essence does not measure up to the "right essences." They have come to realize, ineluctably, the existentialist maxim that *existence precedes essence*: their organic being is not assembled, or disassembled, by analysis or reason; their identity is, however much thrown into the world, irreducible to objective conditions. They are not aspiring to be a thing cis people tolerate as an aberrant guest in their structured, bifurcated world. By transitioning, a person embodies the spontaneity of living their own singular existence without regard for unreal limitations. I admire the existential self-identification that some trans people share with some cis people as well, and trans people seem to me just as, or possibly *more* likely, to realize themselves as anyone.[29]

Before I examine more subtle and complicated differences and similarities between cis and trans people in the following chapters, I would like to pause a moment and ask, how can we label the phenomenon I am describing?

*

Every kind of science relies on taxonomy, the observation of *mere* difference. I emphasize "mere" because in responsible, objective scientific taxonomy, there is nothing metaphysically or socially entailed by an organism's different form, whether apprehended in sensory appearance or biochemical makeup. These differences are not *essential* meaning, however; they are not issued from or connected to a hidden intrinsic substance. They are circumstantial, nominal, and provisional. (Taxonomies, while stable and given, are not predetermined or externally justified.) Meanings come when others look at mere difference, morphological or otherwise, and interpret it to entail something social, sexual, or psychological besides its own forms.[30] Taxonomy, moreover, is a significant methodological component of queer theory and third-wave feminism—the proliferation of inclusive nonbinary labels (which I discuss shortly), the celebration of individuality and uniqueness, and the critical eye that sees the intersections between gender, sex, and race—all depend on an acknowledgment and appreciation of the undeniable differences that exist between each of us.[31] In the context of dating cis-het men, I can fully appreciate the historical and social reasons for distrusting and suspecting *their* often toxic taxonomies—and cis men need to be held accountable for this and do their part to rectify it. But in terms of general logic, it seems to be contradictory to impose taxonomy in queer political contexts but then again repudiate taxonomy in romantic contexts.

If we allow for *mere* difference (taxonomy, labeling), and if we can stipulate that it may not be inherently or de jure pernicious to have an affinity for trans people, what are the options that remain?[32] The most popular term these days, it seems, is "trans-attracted." This term inspires a resounding indifference in me. The word is very mechanistic; it maintains a crystal-clear boundary standing between the subject and the object of attraction. The "chaser" watching his "shemale" porn is attracted to the trans-woman-object, but that is not love—in which the wall between lover and beloved comes tumbling down. I propose the simple, and not novel, term that at least carries this valence—*transam*, as an adjective, or as a noun.[33]

The term *transam* has etymological meaning. As an adjective, it is a shortened form of *transamorous*. The noun *transam* combines two words. *Trans* is a truncation of *trans person*. Grammatically, the accusative case denotes the object of the Latin verb *amāre*, to love. The portmanteau *transam* forms a substantive, and refers to a person who loves, or feels amorously toward, or an affinity for, a trans person or trans people generally.[34] Whether feelings about one or more specific trans person can be appropriately classified into a phenomenon and, if so, whether there are ethical quandaries involved in a cis experience of the phenomenon, remains for me to argue in the following pages. However the term transam is deliberately capacious. It makes no assumptions about a person other than that this person is attracted to a trans person or has an affinity for trans people. It is also not exclusive; it adds but a layer to the diverse assemblage of labels we may simultaneously apply to ourselves. It does not encapsulate an entire or exclusive sexual identity. Transams may share Serano's sentiment that "while I find trans women to be extremely hot, I have no desire to limit my dating pool to just trans women" (2013: 103). It is descriptive, yes, but not defining. Transam coexists as a marker of identity alongside, I contend, other identities like queer, straight, monogamous or polyamorous, trans or cis; which is not to say they are equivalent or equally problematic, but to say these distinctions are not necessarily mutually incoherent.

Some argue that our postmodern world is confounded by excessively distinguishing identities,[35] and that we must pare the tree of distorting proliferations.[36] As of now, to take the most obvious example, the acronym LGBT has helped organize a vast number of people who do not identify with historical cissexual and monosexual majorities.[37] Like every other acronym, however, this one reduces accuracy and nuance for the sake of convenience. Amended versions have sprung up: with LGBTQIA, are added queer, intersex, and asexual. Alternatively, others acknowledge BMNOPPQ[38] as a workable acronym under which previously effaced gender and sexual identities can find a place for purposes of activism and community organizing. The letters stand for bisexual, multisexual, no-label, omnisexual, pansexual, polysexual, and Q as "experientially bisexual folks who primarily identify as queer."[39] It is perhaps inelegant,[40] but it at least gives non-monosexual people a way to label their *mere* difference; it does not pigeonhole them into some label that does not resonate, which can be dehumanizing and infuriating.[41]

In her book *Excluded,* Serano defends the use of "bisexual" as an umbrella term under which non-monosexual people may be categorized, pointing out several more nuanced meanings the term conveys. Her points are valid. More important for us, she announces that "labels like pansexual and omnisexual (which imply attraction to everyone) do not personally resonate with me, because they seem to erase a difference that I experience" between men and women.[42] Serano describes her primary attraction to women, which she experiences more deeply and emotionally, as opposed to her occasional attraction to men, which tends to be less comfortable but occasionally exciting and novel.[43] *Bisexual,* she contends, is a reasonably accurate label for this kind of sexuality, where the masculine and feminine are legitimately on the table as sexual objects.

How does this relate to relationships between cis and trans people, specifically the love a cis man has for a trans woman?

For a number of people on both sides of these relationships, the label of bisexual does not feel right. While bi and queer trans women certainly exist in significant numbers, they often socialize in predominantly queer spaces: queer parties, activist groups, intellectual circles, or art/social collectives,[44] But many trans women, including most of my friends and lovers, socialize in mainly hetero-centric or not-queer spaces, with cis-het men their main romantic and sexual interest. Likewise, cis men, whose primary social circles are hetero-centric, but who are sexually and romantically interested in trans women, seldom identify as bisexual. The latter results perhaps from latent homophobia—a reluctance to be associated with homosexuality in any way—but mostly it is because they truly relate to trans women *as women*; they feel there is nothing "bi" about it.[45]

To me, to embrace the term bisexual suggests being bi-romantic, that is, regularly attracted to intimacy and romantic contact with men as I am with women. Although I have had sex with men, the label "bisexual," to quote Serano again, "does not personally resonate with me, because [it] seem[s] to erase a difference that I experience" between men and women. Therefore, I cannot deny that *technically* the term bisexual applies to me, but it just does not feel like an accurate descriptor of my sexuality, which largely revolves around female partners, straight pornography, etc. The aptness of the term queer, and why it has been a productive category for social activism and organization, is the built-in "fuck you" it contains.[46] But "queer" is deliberately vague and nonexclusive; and we are often asked precisely what we mean by it.

Certainly there are bi, pansexual, and other kinds of cis men who are sexually and romantically interested in trans women, and whose circles are queer and progressive. And down the street, there may be a cis, hetero-identified man in a sports bar watching football with his friends, and this guy has had many straight trans women as lovers. So can we cover these two otherwise disparate people under an identity concept—not to pigeonhole them, but to underline some connection that brings them together? This might serve as a basis for some nascent activism,[47] it might perhaps clarify a social phenomenon buried under all kinds of misunderstanding, or it may simply provide the men with a language to discriminate the mere difference of one their preferences from others. And what do these men have in common with a guy who starts falling for a woman, taking her to be cis, who learns she is trans and does not freak out, who follows his heart and stays with her? This man now finds himself in a curious situation he never anticipated. He had taken completely for granted his being hetero; now, in some instances, other heterosexuals and monosexuals have a hard time believing that was ever true.[48] These different kinds of men have little in common sexually except for their shared involvement with trans women. While they might not think much of the connection, outsiders definitely note it and demand an explanation, which, in turn, causes some confusion.[49]

Julia Serano, informally surveying a number of cis men she either chatted with online or went on dates with, found no reason to suspect an archetypal thread running through all such men.

> Some said that they found trans women more interesting, open-minded, and/or courageous the average cis woman. Others said they had honestly not considered dating a trans woman before, but they really liked my profile, and they considered themselves to be queer-positive, so they didn't consider my transness to be a big deal. Still others put it quite simply: They are attracted to women, and while most of their past partners were cis women, a few were trans women, and it really makes no difference to them.[50]

Many men interested in trans women are defiantly heterosexual, others are proudly bisexual, some are happily ambiguous ("mostly X + some Y or Z"), and probably a good number don't think about it much and simply follow their urges, hopefully in considerate and respectful ways. (I am not sure how to quantify the distance separating these men from chasers, letches, or abusers, but I insist that in many cases, at least, there is a qualitative difference.) I propose that the term *transam* provides a common reference point for such an amorphous, scattered social group.[51]

I employ the label light heartedly.[52] To be sure, gender, sexual identities, and the labels that describe them are serious existential matters, with effects that can generate significant anxiety. Why then make things even more awkward with loaded, overtly political terms that suggest firm ideological commitments? It is not without irony, or awareness of some discursive tension, that I favor the label *transam*. A trans woman writer, Piper Dawes, has written previously about the term's neutrality. "It is a pansexual term on both sides (any gender attracted to any transgender — [sic] can include relationships with more than one transgender person)."[53] However, the term is open to all kinds of associations and interpretations that may please or mollify those who use it, and since the focus of this book is cis-hetero transamorous men, it may be appropriate to gloss some of the ways they might apply it.

Perry Gruber of the *Transamorous Network* writes about how he finds some lighthearted joy in embracing the term for its association with the classic Pontiac Thunderbird car, whose logo was a dramatic Phoenix: "And kind of like that bird, we Transamorous guys are emerging from the cesspool that is social criticism, ostracism and shrinking before social claims that our love is *taboo*, to claim that part of our identity making us uniquely us ... among other things."[54] There is nothing expressly masculine about the term *transam*—since it applies to transamorous femmes just as well, as Dawes argues—but it may help some hetero men overcome insecurities about their masculinity. With these *queer* associations, they can take steps toward a better understanding of themselves and the people to whom they are directly and indirectly connected.

In this book, I address the masculine gender not as an essential substance but as a nominal fragment of true experience. In progressive discourse, gendered expressions of "toxic masculinity" have rightfully become a focus of much social criticism.[55] Yet, most of us have a hard time imagining a world without at least some gendered behaviors.[56] As Serano puts it, "Sometimes, ways of being that resonate with us fit well into societal norms, while other times they may defy such norms.[57] Some cis male transams identify strongly with their masculinity, and, if we may be generous, it may be for reasons deeper than clinging to the privileged position of men in the world's most powerful hierarchies, however real that clinging may well be.

My own sexual orientation is complex (see chapter 7), but I present stereotypically masculine and have never felt much compunction about it. Socialization and privilege explains much, for sure, but is one of many forces at work in the neuronal shaping which determines identity. One noticeable feature of mine is a tall and broad stature, which drew me to sports, fitness, and some of the attendant trappings of masculinity.[58] Geographical location certainly has an influence, as any young trans or transam would experience viscerally the difference between growing up in San Francisco and Missoula. I grew up in the mountains of Colorado, gravitating toward climbing, country music, and cowboy boots. My oldest friends never left cis-het circles.

It is possible, I hope, that masculinity means more than clinging to privilege or internalized homophobia or transphobia. As Serano writes of the female gender, "One would have to have to have a rather grim view of the female population to believe that a majority of us could so easily be 'brainwashed' or 'coerced' into enthusiastically adopting an entirely contrived or wholly artificial set of gender expressions."[59] I agree with Serano that a charitable reading of the two genders, male and female, is possible, just not a metaphysical one about essences. However, I still diverge from Serano's injunction to employ the term bisexual because finding "some alternative label" means that "we would have to start from scratch with new activist terminology (panphobia, poly-invisibility?) to describe how we are marginalized."[60] It is my contention that bisexual identity does not equal *transam* identity; her point about activism is well taken, however, and in that respect we are always running back to the starting point of identity in taxonomy, which I noted above—mere difference is just that, *mere*, barely, hardly. (Consider all the problems wrapped up with the widely circulated acronym LGBT; the trauma which adding the Q implies; and then the expectation to end in a final QIA, where A could stand for Ally or Asexual, depending on whom you ask!)

One reason many transams avoid coming out as transam is because people say, either to their face or to others, "Are you bi?" or, "He's confused."[61] It's astonishing how some people dump on transams, as if their entire life to that point had been a lie and an affront to decent, nondeceptive, cis hetero monosexuals.[62] Lives have been ruined by shame-police who see otherwise innocent—a crucial and implicit caveat throughout my discussion—transamory as a sickness because they see trans people as sick and because they perceive a threat to their own entitlement.[63] Paring down the number of labels available to us would be a mistake, in my opinion. It would almost feed into the mentality of those who demand we cram ourselves into the homo-bi-hetero trilemma, which is pretty much all they are comfortable with—with trans identities altogether under vicious attack by legislators and policymakers. It seems to me the proliferation of sexual and gender identities (genderqueer, genderfucker, multisexual, etc.) has done more good than harm for opening up spaces where more people can feel comfortable as part of an interconnected social fabric—spaces wherein they do not have to hide.[64] Yet no extant terminology has the same disarming effect for transams, who are a heterogeneous population.[65]

Of course, the proliferation of terms can lead to confusion. But with smartphones at our hips, we can look up the meaning of any acronym at any time and easily disambiguate unfamiliar terms. We should not be in any hurry to call an end to this current age of proliferating nomenclature. Each new label is a refinement, not a cluttering. People have and do label transams as bisexual, or sexually confused, as if those terms had a direct line to some objective reality. But when a new term cuts into the dance, it weakens the illusion that such terms denote some fixed referent that can be summed up so conveniently.

The proliferation of terms creates confusion where there should be confusion. We should never presume certainty when we peer into the black box of another's sexuality or gender expression. Moreover, the proliferation of terms reminds us that our identities are not discrete essences; they are dynamic constellations of causes, conditions, volitions, and impulses. They exist, and we speak of them; but they exist nominally, as shifting fields we attempt to pin a few labels on to understand and communicate. Not only is language provisional, moreover, our own *self* is nominal; we never find the rock it completely hides under. Our journey through self-creation refines the description of our experience. We may find the term transam to be a gate more than an obstacle. The following chapter reviews contemporary and classical theories that look behind the veil of sexual and gender essences to expose a free and open space.

REFRAMING GENDER AND SEXUAL IDENTITIES

THE BUDDHIST PATH AND THE TRANSAM

Naomi Scheman has floated the maxim "Transsexual lives are lived, hence livable" (Scheman 1997). Most writers and activists working on trans issues have tried to make lives more livable by analyzing what stands in the way of that livability and by imagining paths to its enhancement. Like its relative, feminism,[1] transgender theory and practice begins with an actually and historically oppressed position and then proceeds to analyze the source of oppression, imagine its transformation, and devise methods for resisting it.[2] Since making a life (more) livable parallels the Four Noble Truths in Buddhism, I will use a Buddhist scaffolding, which I believe welcomes all kinds of interpolations from the field of transgender studies. In gender theory, sex and gender undeniably *appear*, but it is not clear whether to annihilate them, essentialize them, or criticize them yet let them stand in a weakened form. Just so, the central concern of Buddhist metaphysics is how to avoid turning the undeniable *appearance* of a Self into an essential metaphysical category that locks us into an anxious existential destiny.

1) The Truth of Suffering
After spending years in arduous contemplation, Siddhartha Gautama wandered into town from the woods. As he carried himself impressively, people asked what spiritual information he had acquired. His first teaching was that living as we ordinarily

do is painful. Pains are often injuries and illnesses, felt alone or with others. They traditionally fall under the category of "the suffering of suffering" or "suffering upon suffering."[3]

Even when we do not feel pain, we constantly worry about losing the feeling of health and well-being. Trans people and transams may be anxious about humiliation or degradation; they may fear diminishing their social capital in whatever positions they hold.[4] We all fear missing the people we love, or of changing so much that it will become difficult to recognize ourselves.[5] In Buddhist terminology, it is the "suffering of change."

Even in a moment of calm, it could happen that a wave of melancholy overcomes us, and we intuit something amiss or awry. This is called "all-pervasive suffering"[6] or "the suffering of everything composite."[7] No doubt, one privilege of privilege is the ability to push these "unwarranted" fears aside. Indeed, many people live mostly comfortable, fulfilling lives until conditions (sickness, old age, death) inevitably bring manifest pain their way. The Tibetan Buddhist teacher, Gampopa, explains in his twelfth-century masterpiece *The Jewel Ornament of Liberation* that while some people seem bothered by acute pain and blatant loss, they are, in fact, deferring a more pervasive existential suffering by burying their heads in the sand and failing to acknowledge the impermanent composition of reality. For the comfortable and contented, any sense of ennui or alienation remains a nearly imperceptible irritation, like an eyelash dangling before their eye. For the sensitive and the inquisitive, it is as if that eyelash has fallen into their eye. They are aware of it everywhere they look; the pain is not oppressive, and they can enjoy the moment despite the irritant. This nagging but not fully accessible feeling of having an eyelash in one's eye resonates in numerous first-person accounts of trans identity.[8]

In brief, Buddhist tradition names three "marks of existence": impermanence, unsatisfactoriness, and lack of essence.[9] The point of the Buddha's teaching about suffering through change, disappointment, and meaninglessness is not, however, to despair in the acceptance of pain but, rather, to examine its various causes.

2) The Truth of the Cause
Following his unexpected teaching about life's basic—and basis in—pain, the Buddha offered an equally counterintuitive diagnosis of its cause. The cause is attachment, in the sense of fixating, latching onto. Naturally, we seek to increase pleasure and avoid pain. But that search presupposes an even more primary desire—a wish or fantasy to possess a stable identity of being (self or ego) that endures the vicissitudes of reality consistently unfolding before it. Clinging to every shred of stability, change frustrates us. We long to stand on firm ground. To an essential, fixed reference point, all those random occurrences and unpredictable fluctuations of existence appear wildly threatening, so we build walls to keep them out, guarding our egos anxiously and angrily. Contemporary Buddhist scholar Mark Siderits writes apropos:

> Existential suffering arises from the assumption that there is a "me" for whom events can have significance. Such suffering arises out of the suspicion that the kind of meaning we want is not to be had, that our best efforts at attaining happiness will inevitably be frustrated. And we experience suffering because this seems like such an affront to the dignity of the being we take ourselves to be. Now suppose it could be shown that while there are the experiences that make up a lifetime, those experiences have no owner. There is no "me" whose experiences they are. In that case the conviction that my life should have uniquely special significance to me would turn out to be based on a mistake. For experiences in my life to have meaning, there must be more than just the

experiences, there must be something separate from them for which they have good or bad meanings. *Without belief in a separate self, existential suffering would no longer arise. Such suffering requires belief in something whose demand for meaning and significance is violated.* It requires belief in a self (26-27, emphasis mine).

Moreover, belief in the essential self carries over to other essential qualities or characteristics of the self. So alongside the self, we affirm the essence of Man and Woman. Whether essential qualities are taken to be a possession or an aspiration, we suffer when those qualities are threatened or unmet. Manhood and Womanhood, we imagine, occupy a fixed reference of gender in a galaxy around which reality swirls. It follows that sexual orientation, too, has essential qualities (gay-bi-straight). As I advocated in chapter 1, the truth of the cause can help us to frame sexual and gender identity with more inclusion and nuance.

3) The Truth of Cessation
Now that the Buddha has diagnosed the cause of suffering, he imagines an alternative. What if the cause itself were to be extirpated? What would happen if the walls protecting the cause came down, if we allowed that sense of self and its attributes to exist by the same logic as the rest of reality: impermanent, composite, conditioned, unmoored by any absolute certainty? Perhaps it would be like gaining consciousness within a bad dream—though images and feelings that populate our experience would not disappear, the suffering they cause would sting less; and we might allow these appearances to come and go, like a name written on water, the path of a bird in flight, or a snake untying its own knots.[10] When it comes to our embodied or interpersonal experience, so often guided by the ideological fixtures of sexuality and gender, what if these were dispelled, not just intellectually as the result of mulling over theory, but experientially so that

we might stop looking over our shoulders for approval or reprimand. Serano describes an epistemological shift she underwent in the event of her transition:

> The taken-for-granted assumption that female and male were fixed and reliable states suddenly appeared to me to be the product of a mass hallucination, held together only by the fact that so few people actually had the firsthand experience of transitioning—of seeing how such small differences in one's physical gender can result in such a large difference in the way one is perceived and treated by others (2007: 217).

So too, I contend, the cis-het transam could undergo shifts in belief—indeed, in how he believes altogether—once he relinquishes assumptions regarding his mythical Manhood and male essence alongside his paragon's *feminine mystique*, in the influential second-wave feminist Betty Friedan's felicitous phrase.

4) The Truth of the Path
The fourth and final truth that the Buddha teaches is how to achieve the wakefulness imagined in the third Noble Truth. He offers no magic bullet. Rather, it takes great effort and work to leave "the hut of ordinary mind," which has been the seat of so much suffering and anxiety.[11] The truth of the path points to an array of resources that could help us deconstruct our false sense of having a permanent, coherent self. The resources are employed in three ways: *learning* denotes acquiring information; *contemplating* essays discerning, analyzing and synthesizing, finding patterns and problems; and *meditating* temporarily, intensively suspends all of that perception and cognition, savoring the subtle new flavor of noticing—but not retaining or holding onto—things which pass transiently in the wake of any learning and contemplating.[12] The Buddhist canon's hundreds of volumes, its tens of thousands of commentaries, and

the infinite oral traditions and experiential techniques fit into this schematic. Theories in this tradition do not compete for intellectual impressiveness so much as therapeutic efficacy. It is trying to release the self from its captivity in an illusory selfhood by examining how suffering is the result of causality. The Four Noble Truths supply us with usable frameworks for understanding sexual orientation and gender identity.[13]

*

It is imperative for me to note that trans people face systemic oppression and they are also murdered at alarming rates.[14] These imminent threats to their survival are good reason to defer any theorization or intellectualization to activist political organizing, and some trans discourse argues that trans people should not be subjected to treatment as theoretical objects.[15] Nor, I imagine, would trans people eagerly seek a theoretical cure to soothe any fantastical anxieties when the risks of transitioning are far from intangible to them.

Yet here, I think, is the rub. The Four Noble Truths begin with the recognition that transition of any kind implies transience. It calls into question whatever (ego, group, society) defends its survival beyond physical wellbeing. What is the reality of something like *identity*? How can an *identity* be threatened, or taken away (in the sense not of "stolen" as a financial misdeed, but of exterminated)? Perhaps it cannot be taken away from a subjective experience, since my own perspective is indubitable, but it is taken away in objective terms all of the time, whether by ourselves through initiative or by external factors.[16] For example, the gender a person as assigned at birth is not essential, as by the definition transitioning would presuppose. Trans people must face directly—and they cannot necessarily afford to speculate about—this transitory, if not perpetually chang*ing* then, at a minimum, spontaneously change*able*, feature of gender.

The Noble Truths are not derived as the logical conclusion from valid premises like a (deductive) theory is. These truths are extrapolated from experience, at most inductively. Suffering, for instance, is a given phenomenon (with more or less probability and intensity) in our plain experience of reality—we might stub a toe or get humiliated. But pain does not expose some ontological or objective feature of the cosmos. To be sure, the Buddha's extrapolation does involve at least some theoretical principles, makes cognitive statements, but so too does all practice in some regards (no matter their origins, even art and music involve theories).[17] Theory may, however, be carried lightly and still provide us with a framework, such as the taxonomy I broached in chapter 1, in order to understand the dynamic ranges of impermanent identities. Thus we find, in the Second Noble Truth, that we have a default theory that secures ourselves by clinging to inviolable essences. But since our experience of reality is not entirely coherent and reliable, the default theory attaching to a stable, solid self amidst the flowing stream of causation has the propensity to *aggravate* suffering. We might as well accept that our existence depends on a vast array of external conditions that are, themselves, arbitrary and groundless. And yet to dream of a final escape from the cycle of rebirth as in the Third Noble Truth could possibly amount to an immature fantasy, and to detach from the fight against oppression and accept life's randomness is not what a class of people fearing for their survival would be most helped to hear.

We can make the step from the Second to Third Noble truth if we consider a simple point. We cannot possibly avoid treating others as objects so long as we refer to our own selves, or anything, as essential. It could seem, though this point I make tentatively, that the trans person could deflect objectification precisely *because* of her or his self's non*essential* gender identity. This is not to say that identification with gender is completely unreal. It is simply to point out that gender identity is not predetermined, foregone, and necessary by anything other than the subject who identifies with it as his/her/their own. That identity might never have once changed, for it may have been true from the very first moment of consciousness that someone assigned the label of a boy identifies as a girl, or vice versa. The problem is that our default theory of a stable self denies the *transient*—in the sense of transferable—qualities of identity, and the trans person who considers their trans identity to be inviolable and isolated from other gendered experiences leans on the default theory. What I wonder is how we could *not* treat others ultimately as objects for as long as we insist on owning a self with essential, absolute and immutable qualities.

The problem for anyone operating under the default theory, I contend, is an attachment to essence that obscures the Second Noble Truth, the cause of suffering, which is to desire something other than reality's contingent nature. Perhaps you may proceed with a firm conviction that you have a self, and sexuality and gender would play a large role in it. So too a man thinks he possesses an identity, and when he meets a woman, he judges her according to the same conditioned codes that defend his own claim to have a self; and the woman either accords or does not to *his* sense of self. In the West, Plato and Aristotle offered theories, indeed taxonomies, of the soul—wherein men, women, children, and slaves are what they are *essentially*, by virtue of the *type* of soul they possess.[18] Augustine folded the Greek notion of souls into Christian theology and provided the West with its discourse on identity for twenty centuries. Augustine dictated that men and women appear as men and women because these are the expressions of an underlying metaphysical source: manhood or masculinity and womanhood or femininity. There is an unobstructed correlation between Being as such and the expression of Being. The gender and sexuality discernible in existence are so determined by their fundamental essence. Those beings whose existence does not conform to an essence are labeled abnormal. The advantage of this theory is that it reassures us that what we *desire*—namely, our self-identity—is not illusory but, rather, is undergirded by metaphysical reality.[19]

This theoretical orientation is not only intellectualism; it is inscribed in the flesh. Someone who destabilizes a norm or transgresses a code risks receiving physical harm. When a woman (or "woman") subverts the messages that organize the way a man blithely and blindly makes his way through the social world, the subsequent disorientation he feels could throw him into a lethal rage; a terrifying example of it is in the film *Boys Don't Cry*, based on real events. Our culture and social institutions are built on the foundation of this theory of the masculine and the feminine essence. "Marriage" essentially unifying one man and one woman is a stubborn institution, which remains to be queered. Because our social institutions are pervaded by this kind of theory, cis men are perhaps sometimes uneasy in their relationships with trans women and do not treat them with the dignity that would be accorded to someone who does not pull the metaphysical rug from under them and their friends and their families.

For trans people and those who care about them, I submit, this pervasive theoretical orientation is toxic. Nevertheless, alternatives *are* hard to come by. A popular option, it seems, is not to overthrow the metaphysics of essence, but to redefine those essences. In the traditional, uncritical model, the soul possesses symbolic physical markers—the genitals are synecdoches of the male or female essence. In its modified form, those symbolic markers are given less significance and the male and female essence become abstract terms filled with faith and conviction. Some branches of second and third wave feminism took this approach and contributed to the rift between cis feminists and trans women.[20] Janice Raymond pulls no punches in her infamous statement, "All transsexuals rape women's bodies by reducing the real female to an artifact, appropriating this body for themselves" (Raymond: 104). Raymond does not try to defend the ontology of Woman as Aristotle and the Church

Fathers have; instead, she redefines womanhood as a *history* of living in a female body since birth. In this elegant deflection, womanhood remains an elusive metaphysical fortress that is inaccessible to trans women.[21]

Raymond's mentor, Mary Daly, a writer of singular lyrical talent, limns the *narrativity* of an essential "Female Self" in *Gyn/Ecology: The Metaethics of Radical Feminism*:

> Since women have a variety of strengths, and since we have all been damaged in a variety of ways, our yes-saying assumes different forms and *is* in different degrees. In some cases it is clear and intense; in other instances it is sporadic, diffused, fragmented. Since Female-identified yes-saying is complex participation in be-ing, since it is a Journey, a process, there is no simple and adequate way to divide the Female World into two camps: those who say "yes" to women and those who do not . . . It is she, and she alone, who can determine how far, and in what way, she will/can travel. She, and she alone, can dis-cover the mystery of her own history, and find how it is interwoven with the lives of other women (xlvi-xlvii).

Despite the veneer of existential freedom suggested by the prose, Daly retains a Catholic flavor in her conceptions of ontological essence. This is evinced in her judicious employment of capital letters for nouns she indexes to ontologically heavier, more-real conceptual objects. For example, she writes, "*Self* is capitalized when I am referring to the authentic center of women's process, while the imposed/internalized false "self," the shell of the Self, is in lower case" (26). Her capitalized Self—that "authentic center of women's process"—is simply ontologically foreclosed to trans women. Trans women, according to her, cannot "dis-cover the mystery of her own history" through existential realization. Rather, the trans woman is like a species of cyborg, a shell housing no true Female Self.[22]

Numerous theorists such as Sandy Stone and Thalia Mae Bettcher have interrogated such implicit gender essentialism, providing critical alternatives, but their writing takes some effort.[23] It seems easier to fall back on old ideologies of essence and to speak with vague conviction about the essentially gendered "spirit."[24] Sheila Jeffreys also denies there is such a thing as Woman-essence; however, she does claim that "transgenderism" *in toto* adheres to this very mistaken view of gender. While it is *sometimes* true (see chapter 3), it is irresponsible to universalize cases where individual trans people may essentialize sexuality and gender identity based on uncritical metaphysics (Jeffreys 2014).

It should be noted that this metaphysics is not unique to the West. Confucianism holds dearly to male and female essences and social roles entailed by those essences; the Indian *Laws of Manu* thrive off of a strict essential classification of human kinds.

So then what alternatives are available? One thing that led to the writing of this book was the observation when I was younger of some cis hetero men I knew who were struggling to navigate a romantic, sexual, even platonic relationship with trans women. This was an experience I did not share, and I could not help but wonder why. The more I thought about it, the more I believed it mattered what theoretical orientation you bring to the situations and people you encounter. I noticed so much talk about "real man" and "real woman"; about marriage and procreation; and about sexual ethics dictating that a man should do this and a woman should do that. It was foreign to me because I was not exposed to the Christian tradition. At fifteen, I became fascinated with Buddhism and immersed myself in it. The Indo-Tibetan tradition was my preference then and since. When I first encountered trans women a few years later, I was not framing it in metaphysical terms. My lenses spared me the trauma I witnessed others suffer. And one of the most useful ideas I found was in the theory of the Five Aggregates.

THE FIVE AGGREGATES THEORY AND TRANS DISCOURSE

As we have now seen, the Buddhist tradition asks: "If the self is such a problem, what is it? Where is it?" The same question is raised about sex in the transgender context. According to Thalia Mae Bettcher, trans discourse is engaged in a tug-of-war between two major paradigms. One, perhaps best represented by Judith Butler is built around the notion that genders, and even biological sexes, are entirely socially constructed categories; they are discursive, nominal labels, not grounded in any substance, whether the material body or an immaterial soul. Jay Prosser, representing the contrasting paradigm, argues this notion of performative identity devalues trans self-identities because it suggests that trans people are conjuring their identities out of thin air. They would rather establish that these identities emanate from some metaphysical source like the body, which gives rise to what seems like an essential, soul-like identity.[25] Since these considerations are central to Indian Buddhist theory, we might draw on the latter to breathe some fresh air into contemporary transgender discourse.[26]

After the European Enlightenment, scientific experimentation was privileged over abstract speculation, and it became less acceptable to ignore the material body in favor of the immaterial soul. Subsequently, more nuanced critiques of the metaphysical primacy of the body were developed by Nietzsche, Freud, and others. In Prosser's influential book *Second Skins*, he defends the body as the dynamic site of transgender identity:

> Relating first how the body comes to be marked by sex wrongly, then how it comes to be marked correctly, transsexual narratives take up poststructuralism's

untellable story. What makes it possible for a female-to-male transsexual to name the somatic material (skin, tissue, and nerves) transplanted from his forearm or his abdomen to his groin "my penis," or for a male-to-female transsexual to name the inverted remains of her penis "my vagina" is a refiguring of the sexed body that takes place along corporeal, psychic, and symbolic axes. Gendered becoming, becoming a man or a woman, occurs for the transsexual at these points of intersection, complex crossings for sure but the investment of sex in the flesh is undeniable. Narratives that immerse us (subject and reader alike) in the bodily matter of sexual difference, transsexual autobiographies challenge theory's cynicism over identity's embodiment. In that s/he seeks to align sex with gender identification; in that the somatic progression toward these goals of sexed embodiment constitutes the transsexual narrative, the transsexual does not approach the body as an immaterial provisional surround but, on the contrary, as the very "seat" of the self. For if the body were but a costume, consider: why the life quest to alter its contours? (Prosser: 67)

Buddhist theory grapples directly with the motivations we have to say "I" and "mine," or "my penis" and "my vagina," while rejecting the full presence of *real* being. Just as there is no uncreated Creator so too there is no unconditioned identity. Yet, there is some voice that pronounces "I" and "mine."[27] It is a voice that is always active and self-assuring, providing us with reference points to organize experience. This undeniable *appearance* of self is called the *pudgala*, "the person." It is not taken for granted as a coherent entity, however, and becomes the object of relentless interrogation. The *pudgala* resembles the general sense of self in Prosser's account.

Searching for a seat of the self, Buddhist theorists distinguish five categories where it might reside, called The Five Aggregates (Sanskrit: *skandhas*). They are: 1) form 2) feeling 3) perception 4) volition 5) consciousness. The question guiding the analysis is whether the constant first-person reference we have in a self is the same as or different than the collection of these aggregates. Buddhist theorists conclude there is no self essentially independent from the aggregates. Indeed, clinging to the self and craving its possessions beyond the mere aggregates is, in fact, the very cause of suffering. For no essence outstrips conditional existence. We ordinarily, superficially assume that something *possesses* our sundry attributes. However, upon closer investigation, we discover that our self cannot be identified except in relation to those same attributes it putatively surpasses. Buddhist teachers conclude that these subtle aggregates encompass the whole range of first-person experience, including sexed and gendered identities.

Aggregate 1) **Form** *(Sanskrit:* rūpa*):*
Buddhist analysis begins with the feeling that our self dwells in the body. We might ask, crudely, where the self literally resides in the body. Maybe the self is located in the brain, or in the heart, or in the belly? Yet we feel our self distributed throughout the body, as when a thorn punctures our foot and our attention shoots there. We are as present there as in the vat of our cerebrospinal fluid. Sometimes our self seems diffused even into the surroundings, as in sexual activities, when our cellular composition is abuzz and the self's energy is coursing not only throughout our own bodies but between another (or others) as well. In these experiences, is there a unifying consciousness that synthesizes diverse sensations in the body's different parts? We might contrast our living bodies with a cadaver no longer mysteriously animated by a soul or self. Once my own body is ground into the earth or ashes, it would lose its self entirely; for "I" had somehow been suspended in or emerged from

"my" bodily frame, that peculiar arrangement of blood, bones, and other chemicals. The embodied self is intuited, but evades analysis. Present one moment, and a simple event (a seizure, an accident) expunges the self for good.

In a similar respect, contemporary gender theory has extensively explored the relationship between the body and the (sexed and gendered) self and has reached a kind of impasse. In Bettcher's terms, the "wrong-body paradigm" seems to affirm the self as identical to the aggregate of form—it is inconceivable except as embodiment, with all its sexed and gendered attributes—while the "transgender paradigm" asserts that the self (with its sexed and gendered attributes) must be something more than the aggregate of form, and attention must be paid to the relationship between the objective body and its subjective flavors or epiphenomena. Judith Butler points in the latter direction:

> It must be possible to concede and affirm an array of "materialities" that pertain to the body, that which is signified by the domains of biology, anatomy, physiology, hormonal and chemical composition, illness, age, weight, metabolism, life and death. None of this can be denied. But the undeniability of these "materialities" in no way implies what it means to affirm them, indeed, what interpretive matrices condition, enable and limit that necessary affirmation . . . [Materiality is] the "that without which" no psychic operation can proceed, but also . . . that on which and through which the psyche also operates.[28] (1993: 66-67)

Butler is skeptical of the unmediated meaningfulness of the material body divorced from the subjectivity that interprets the body's materiality—it is not really a self without the peculiar ingredient of subjective interpretation. The Five Aggregates theory suggests a similar kind of aspiration to track the elusive self, and therefore carefully peels back the intricate layers of subjectivity.

Aggregate 2) **Feeling** *(vedanā) &*
Aggregate 3) **Perception** *(saṃjñā)*
Feeling, as one of the Five Aggregates, refers less to complex emotional states than to basic sensations of good, bad, and neutral. The naked body of blood and bones is reactive: it breaks, it tears open, it withdraws in disgust. It must negotiate the context into which it is thrown, scratching rough surfaces, regurgitating indigestible substances—also caressing soft fabric, tasting fine cuisine. In response to stimuli, sensations of pleasure, pain, and disinterest inexorably arise of their need. Having a self depends on these sensations. The geology of the body—its parts and configuration—affects the way it meets and connects to other bodies. Sexual attraction, for instance, is caught in a matrix of the eroticized body. The body reacts to a combination of appearances. Somewhere in this web of body and emotion, identities form and differences play out.

The Buddhist teacher Chögyam Trungpa writes of this reactive body's process as it metabolizes impinging forces:

> It is like in rock climbing when you insert a metal peg. That is the feeling. But to continue climbing you have to have a rope running through that peg. The rope which you have running though the pegs is perception, the third *skandha* . . . a common link, a common thread that runs between happiness and sadness of body and mind. Perception is based on that which is manifested by form and feeling and that which is not manifested by them. These are the two basic qualities in perception. In the first case, something is manifested via the six sense organs.[29] You perceive something and you relate to it; you relate with that content. That is the first touching and feeling process. Feeling is like

a radiator radiating out. With that radiation, perception takes place as the radiation begins to function as definite details of that and this (Trungpa 26-27).

A body arranged a certain way, encounters another body arranged a different way, and a reaction ensues. There is aversion, attraction or indifference; mental events proliferate; phenomena are named; a more solid sense of self comes to the fore, with its combination of needs and desires. But life is not lived on this level of simple reactivity; we are not anemones responding to stimuli. The aggregates of form, feeling, and perception together do not fulfill what we call our self, especially not our complex, coded, sexed and gendered selves. We can explore further.

Aggregate 4) **Volition** *(samskāra)*
A more complex rendering of the self makes the body more important, not less. In the life of the body, first we are small, and it conditions our experience of the world in every way. As we develop our bodies, they become hypersensitive instruments. We make adjustments. There is reactivity at every level. Learning how our bodies react to the rest of the world, we make choices to push away what causes pain and to grasp what feels good. This is the fourth aggregate, *samskāra*, which can be translated as "volitions"[30] or "mental dispositions."[31]

> [Samskāra] enables the ego to gather further territory, further substance, more things . . . it has the sense of a gathering or accumulation, meaning specifically a tendency to accumulate a collection of mental states as territory (Trungpa: 40).

These volitions or mental dispositions include gross and subtle desires that motivate us to act, to attract pleasurable stimuli and to reject painful ones. Volitions direct aggregates outside and inside the body, defining its boundaries and expressing its drives. Even though reactive, these movements seem to revolve around a kernel of an independent being, and the picture of an enduring quality comes to light, a witness to the unfolding drama—the fifth aggregate is called consciousness.

Aggregate 5) **Consciousness** *(*vijñāna*)*

According to the traditional Buddhist analysis, consciousness is not an autonomous substance, free subject, or pure being.[32] Consciousness integrates the other aggregates. We are conscious *of* some content, be they objects, feelings, or volitions (desires). In search of his own "self," the philosopher David Hume could admit to finding only "impressions," discrete cognitions with specific contents. The "self," he concluded, was just a name he gave to the whole tapestry of impressions, but remained itself unobservable.

On consciousness, Trungpa makes the following observation.

> Consciousness is that sort of fundamental creepy quality that runs behind the actual living thoughts, behind the samskāras. The explicit thoughts, the samsk ras are the actual grown-up thoughts, so to speak; whereas the thoughts produced by consciousness are the undergrowth of those thoughts. They act as a kind of padding. The whole pattern of psychology works in such a way that it is impossible for the explicit thoughts ... to be suspended in nowhere, without any context whatsoever. The subconscious thoughts make the context that is necessary for the explicit ones. ... They are in a sense a kind of kindling. ... So consciousness constitutes an immediately available source of occupation for the momentum of the [aggregates] to feed on (63).

The self is none other than the ongoing interplay of the five aggregates, not something that transcends them. Self can neither provide an "authentic center of women's process" nor assert the superiority of an Alpha Male. The objects of consciousness (feeling, perception, and volition) fluctuate, depending on material conditions, themselves unstable and unpredictable.[33]

*

The writer Julia Serano offers in *Whipping Girl*, now published in a second edition (2016), what she calls an "*intrinsic inclinations model* to explain human gender and sexual variation" (2007: 99), a model she modifies and elaborates on in *Excluded* (2013).[34] As a research biologist and trans woman, Serano is troubled both by the dogmatic conflation of biological difference with identity and by theories that deny the role of biology. Paying close attention to the objective materiality of the body as well as to its subjective interpretations, Serano, whose theorizing is guided by her existential situation, asserts that biology no more naturally determines gender than society socializes us into gender.

Serano cites cases that may suggest a hard-wired seat of sex and gender, including that of David Reimer, who suffered an accidental surgical loss of his penis as an infant and was raised female, but who throughout his life identified as male despite hormone therapy and aggressive socialization as a girl. There are many such cases, as there are also many cases of identical twins with opposite gender expressions and sexual identities, despite nearly identical genetic material and socialization. The mystery remains unsolved. Serano writes:

> Because no single genetic, anatomical, hormonal, environmental, or psychological factor has ever been found to directly cause any of these gender inclinations, we can assume that they are quantitative traits

(i.e., multiple factors determine them through complex interactions). As a result, rather than producing discrete classes (such as feminine and masculine; attraction to women or men), each inclination shows a continuous range of possible outcomes. (99)

Serano thus starts with the existentialist inkling that "like snowflakes or fingerprints, no two people share the exact same gender and sexuality" (2013: 152). To preserve our humanity and dignity, we must respect the absolute uniqueness of individuals.

An additional claim is that "One can never truly peel away the biological from the social or environmental." Brain development shows that brains share a common "architecture—they are made up of neurons (i.e., nerve cells) organized into subregions that specialize in different tasks," but at the same time and certainly in a more distinctive manner compared to other organs, "they are also extraordinarily plastic" (Serrano 2013: 153). For each body, we can track innumerable marks of experience and the intertwining phenomena in, say, learning a language, falling in love, rebounding after a breakup, having a career and/or family. All these relational events and processes affect, or even shape (as neurobiology discovers) the brain, that is, our physically detectable mind.[35]

Serano's theory reveals the elusiveness of sexed and gendered identities due to the remarkable singularities of each "self." Even at the most reduced biological level we can measure the cause of our traits; we find "the function of any given gene or hormone is dependent on the functions of and interactions between countless other different factors." Our bodies' composite elements are not "isolated agents"; each of their performances "within intricate networks" has a "probabilistic rather than deterministic" function (Serano 2013: 161–62). Even the material conditions at their source, as we understand it, do not mark signals of a certain identity. Masculine and feminine identities are not indexed to genitals or chromosomes. Certain arrangements of complex factors yield certain expressions, which are not the issue of essences.

While the self may not be as metaphysically grounded as we once thought, it *can* still be respected. There is no denying we feel alive and suffer vividly. The sense of having a self seems to hold up, especially when we are weary, or on a roll. However, analyzing the self, along with all its taken-for-granted characteristics, exposes it for what it really is, which is not necessarily what we think of it. Placed under the microscope of critical analysis, the self will not evaporate; but it could feel like catching red-handed a thief who has been pilfering goods for a long time. In order words, it is hard to catch sight of the self not simply because it is elusive but, because it is furtive. We seem to be hiding something from ourselves, and that suggests a dilemma. How could we know what we are hiding from ourselves?

Buddhist theory offers a way to address this dilemma; it tries to reconcile the seeming contradiction between the self decomposed into its aggregates and the self that endures, lives, feels, and acts. Buddhism postulates a theory of Two Truths—conventional and ultimate truth.[36] Conventional truth is the world as it appears to us, with its commonly accepted names and meanings that have been decided by consensus (or coercion) over the long course of history. Conventional truth categorizes Man and Woman to account for apparent physical differences within the species. Of course, conventional truths help to maintain the species, like distinguishing fire and water preserve our homes from burning. Conventions are very often convenient, not inherently bad. They are revisable, and we can refine them, sometimes with precision in the manner of scientific knowledge accruing testable hypotheses, other times with different purposes in mind. In ethics, we find ways to treat others with more humanity based on an evolving appreciation of individual beings.

The problem is not the appearances or conventions themselves. The problem arises when we invest conventions with the status of an unassailable, ultimate reality. This is the mistake we make, according to the Buddhist Four Noble Truths, when we take the appearance of our self, which is dependent on the Five Aggregates, to be a *real*, unconditioned entity that possesses its own intrinsic reality, or "own-being" (Sanskrit *svabhāva*).

The ultimate truth is that no appearance whatsoever contains such autonomous reality. Ultimate truth is "emptiness" (śūnyatā). This emptiness is not some kind of empty void. It is, rather, emptiness *of* "own-being." Emptiness does not empty appearance of its reality. To the contrary, it sees through appearance in the *reality* of emptiness. In fact, emptiness accepts, indeed welcomes, the multiplicity of appearances, the multifarious surface of reality. Thus, we arrive at an understanding of the ultimate truth by *thoroughly examining the conventional truth* until the ontological bottom falls out of it.[37]

To say it again, the Buddhist analysis of the Five Aggregates hardly annihilates the self; it proposes that the self will appear to emerge from, dependent upon, the five aggregates. And so therefore we can learn more about this emergence of the self from its reflexive features. Sex and gender identity have functions in this self-reflexive self; their ambiguous role is undeniable. Critical analysis seeks to see our identity attributes as they are by freeing the self of false limitations, indeed, a self-imposed destiny that does not necessarily have grounding in truth or fact outside of our attachments to a self, which is conventional, not ultimate.

All beings suffer for the same reason. We impute a false existence, permanence, and coherence to ourselves and impart attributes to that self, including sexed and gendered ones. The insight we gain through critical analysis will undermine the reification of the false self rather than sustain it, and this will affect the way we perceive and treat reality, including the other beings that are a part of it. Here is a relevant dialogue between the Buddhist teacher Chögyam Trungpa and a student (Trungpa 12):

> Student: When you speak of "things as they are," do you mean completely without projections? It is at least theoretically possible to experience things without projections, isn't it?
>
> Trungpa: It is definitely possible to experience things without projections . . . Seeing things as they are is very plain. Because it is so plain, it is colorful and precise. There is no game involved, therefore it is more precise, clearer. It does not need any relative supports; it does not call for any comparisons. That is why the individuality of things is then seen more precisely—because there is no need to compare anything to anything.

The place of others in relation to the self receives consideration in the theory of the Two Truths; moreover, it suggests some ethical implications of the Five Aggregates theory that bear comparison to a contemporary model of sex and gender. Thalia Mae Bettcher has surveyed the currents that dominate transgender discourse when it comes to trans self-identity and claims to the labels of "man" and "woman." One of these currents is the "wrong-body narrative" in which Man and Woman are taken to be metaphysical essences, and which the trans person can hope to access through alterations of surgery and other "passing" strategies such as binding. This model unfortunately subjects the trans person to "reality enforcement"; that is, no matter to what degree a trans woman lives her life as a woman—in a hospital, prison, or shelter—she can be exposed as "anatomically male" and identified as a man. The alternative model is the "transgender model," which elevates self-identification over essences of Man and Woman. A trans woman is a *woman* if she says she is a woman, though she remains, simultaneously, *trans*. The flaw with this model is that it sometimes alienates trans individuals who are not comfortable defining themselves as nonbinary or to mark themselves with the special qualifier "trans"; they would rather just be a *woman*. This is not an easy philosophical problem to solve, so Bettcher takes a commendable approach, which resembles the Buddhist Two Truths theory.

Bettcher contends that if we look at the ways "woman" is used in trans subcultural settings, where the term resists the dominant notion that the identity of a "woman" is indexed to her attributes or traits, we find that the term works adequately as a convention. The labels "woman" and "man" conventionally convey the sexed and gendered features of a living being. The ultimate truth is that these conventional truths, the phenomenal appearances that manifest in our experience, express no hidden essence. Identity labels can be emptied of meaning as quickly as they have been filled with it. Among trans people, there tends to be little confusion about how the labels of "man" and "woman" are used. Most have resolved practically to stop groping for the metaphysical bottom of these terms and appreciate their useable conveniences, however circumscribed.

> [In trans subcultures] all trans women count as women and do so paradigmatically, not marginally. And trans women count as women not owing to a political decision that arises as a consequence of their status as "difficult cases" but owing to the metaphysical facts that accord with the very meaning of the word "man" and "woman" *as deployed in trans subcultures*. That is, from the perspective of trans subculture, the [reality] enforcer who denies that a trans woman is a woman would be *making an error* every bit as much as if he were to call a non-trans woman a man (Bettcher 243).

Moreover, it is possible and desirable to "reject the entire dominant gender system as based on false beliefs about gender and gender practices that are harmful and even oppressive." This is what Buddhist philosophers do: they reject the dominant system that counts on there being a metaphysical essence; they use the same identity labels as everyone else and yet they understand them in different ways, as useful appearances with the illusion of absolute, eternal substantiality. Bettcher counsels that this mental gymnastics can be practiced. Just as we have worked out of theories that organize our lives around "saved" and "sinner" or around "ethers" and "phlogiston." We can also suspect the hypostatized notions of Man and Woman for their literal unreality, and perhaps ultimately their impracticality, their implacable causation of suffering.

The labels of "man" and "woman" are conventions used for navigating a social space; and it may even be difficult for us to manage life without their deployment in some manner. Paradoxically, many trans people adopt the "fixed meanings of gender terms," which take part in the default essence theory. People in trans subcultures spontaneously use these terms with an implicit understanding of their polyvalence, as Buddhists use the term "I" and "me." We can accept the conventionality of the default theory of stable, substantive identities, and then pursue the ultimate emptiness at their core.

THE QUEST FOR VALIDATION

GIVING BODIES DEFINITION

Writing this chapter, which considers the vagina in trans women's discourse and the implications for transamorous men, makes me feel like I am building my own pillory. It is uncomfortable, but I need to disclose my ambivalent thoughts about the sensitive issue of sex-reassignment or sex-confirmation surgery. I submit that when it comes to the *sexed* body, there is nothing there for surgery to "confirm" or "reassign." That is not to say that an individual might not feel *herself* confirmed. However, the language we use in reference to male or female sexuality being "confirmed" or "reassigned" instills a belief in sexual essences that is, on my reckoning, erroneous and even pernicious. Such essentialism cuts off pathways of communication since it demands we agree about what sexual essences exist before we can speak to each other. Therefore, instead of trying to reach a metaphysical consensus, trans discourse is better off abandoning the quest for ontological certainty to focus on accurate phenomenological descriptions of personal experience that are not in the domain of essence-policing.

On previous occasions, trans friends or partners have been puzzled, frustrated, or offended when I've admitted I would hesitate in romantic or sexual attraction to a woman who has had sex-confirmation, or bottom, surgery.[1] This admission bothers me, too, because it suggests my trans-attraction boils down to a phallic fetish. If many of my partners have been cis women, why would I be any less attracted to a women whose vagina is was formed surgically? A rationale such as "If I want a vagina, I prefer a 'real' one" won't satisfy me because of the linguistic and metaphysical fallacies it involves. It requires a more subtle investigation to dispel the fallacious discourse of "real" and "artificial" genitals in the formation of a woman's identity. I do not intend to criticize the choice anyone makes to have surgery; and I do not ascertain an ontological difference between Hormone Replacement Therapy and surgery; however, I do wish to raise skeptical questions about the casual and erroneous linking of genitalia and gender when we begin to enumerate rules about how a body gets sexed. My reluctance to wade into these waters is relieved because I think it will help us to see how words and bodies interplay for trans women and cis men in love.

*

A trans friend of mine recently recounted on Facebook an experience she had at a transgender support group. During the session's recess, an older trans woman approached her and, without even making a proper introduction, asked her "So, are you *complete?*" My friend replied that she was not entirely sure what the older woman meant. The woman's exasperated rejoinder was, "Have you had *all your surgeries?*"

My friend, disingenuously at this point, replied to the invasive question, "I'm not sure what you mean by *all.*"

"Are you SRS or not?" As if this information were essential for any further communication.

Such exchanges reveal that some trans women consider sex-confirmation or reassignment surgery the only way to "complete" the process of transitioning.[2] What motivates upholding this standard? Generally, concepts invested with inviolability tend to rank degrees of truth by their absoluteness. The concept of "Woman," for example, is true for so long or inasmuch as it is comprehensive and definitive. By this conception, a Real Woman obtains some traits and rejects others: she wears makeup, does not interrupt, etc. Having a vagina would appear to be the index of a rightful claim to womanhood. Without making any claims about physiology, I do very much wish to address the words and attitudes this appearance implies.

I have been the romantic partner of trans women considering surgery, rejecting surgery, or rediscovering sexuality after surgery. I do not claim to be an authority on anyone's identity claim, and I certainly do not judge anyone's personal decision. That said, I am involved in the discourse to the extent words and attitudes that inform my lovers' identities can implicate and affect me, sometimes in uncomfortable ways. The issue I address here is the privilege that many grant to essential features of "man" and "woman," which I argue in chapter 2 causes more suffering than reality demands. What I have experienced as uncomfortable is when a trans woman articulates a wish that bottom surgery would confirm her womanhood, not phenomenologically, but metaphysically, because metaphysical beliefs always solicit assent, whereas our personal phenomenologies remain valid in their singularity.

Surveying early transsexual autobiographies from the mid-twentieth century, Sandy Stone notes that many trans women think bottom surgery is the apotheosis of a fantastical woman-essence—where the subjects construct a "specific narrative moment when their personal sexual identification changes from male to female. This moment is the moment of neocolporrhaphy—that is, of gender reassignment, or 'sex change surgery.'" One person wrote: "In the instant that I awoke from the anesthetic, I realized that I had finally become a woman." The subject does not describe what becoming a woman *feels like* (as Simone de Beauvoir does for eight hundred pages in *The Second Sex*); they only announce a metaphysical event that we are not meant to question.

Stone comments on another subject that she "displaces

the irruptive masculine self, still dangerously present within her, onto the God-figure of her surgeon/therapist Werner Kreutz, whom she calls The Professor, or The Miracle Man. ... The female is immanent, the female is bone-deep, the female is instinct. With Lili's complicity, The Professor drives a massive wedge between the masculine and the feminine within her" (Stone 225-226). What trait marks a "real" (trans) woman?

It has never occurred to me that a trans woman with bottom surgery was any more of a woman than one without. My own limited sexual experience with trans women who have had bottom surgery is defined by attitudinal and not physiological (though these, too, may exist) differences. What I have found to be uncomfortable was that, perhaps issuing from the belief in identity as essence, sexuality for most post-bottom surgery women that I have known was restricted to a conventional man=top and woman=bottom paradigm. Any and all erotic energy had to strictly conform to this framework. Frankly, I take this to be the general orientation of a straight "vanilla" female sexuality, cis or trans[3] (a sexuality I have learned over time to avoid getting into erotic situations with) but this attitude only seemed to me exaggerated in these women who had had bottom surgery.

The women I have known with this surgery articulated themselves and acted as if to establish an imaginary essence of womanhood and conform to hetero-normative practices and convictions that could obscure their having transitioned. Some trans people even choose to live "stealth"[4] and who offer understandable reasons for doing so—reasons that are not founded on essentialist metaphysics. For example, an anonymous guest on the blog *That Guy Kas* writes,

> I'm waiting for a world in which being trans has about as much significance as being left-handed or having red hair does, because that's about as much significance

as being trans has to my identity most days. Until then, I remain stealth because I have no interest in letting them take my ability to live as a man—an ability I have paid dearly for—away from me.⁵

The actress Trace Lysette in a 2015 interview with *The Advocate* recalls, during a period of her life when she was living stealth, the murder of another trans woman in New York City:

> She died a block away from my apartment at Harlem Hospital, and I thought to myself, *I'm not doing my trans sisters and brothers any justice by living a semicloseted existence. I need to live out loud and live visibly to help get the respect and the rights we deserve* . . . I thought I was doing the right thing and for a while it was OK, but eventually it got exhausting . . . I wasn't happy compartmentalizing my life. I couldn't be the colorful person I really was inside around the folks who didn't know. I was very depressed. I had muted and censored myself, my struggle and my brilliance.⁶

Lysette's renunciation of stealth is not couched in metaphysical language. She does not describe a vacillation between "becoming a woman" and then veering back toward another plane where she is a "trans woman." Her remarks highlight a personal phenomenology, as well as a clear ethical stance of openness that offers solidarity to other trans women and illumination to cis people. The problem with the accounts Stone critiques is that they sell a metaphysics in which it is important for a trans woman to transcend her transness and then conceal that she is (or *was?*) trans—all thanks to a surgeon's miracle work.

The articulation of our desires projects identity forward into historical time and outward into social space; it is important because the language everyone uses reverberates through culture. I submit the conventional essences we desperately grasp onto, like anchors in rough seas, around sex and gender do more harm than good. As noted in chapter 2, trans women are the targets of harm and oppression in our society. While in no way commensurable, some transam cis men have suffered ostracism from their family, professional discrimination, and physical violence.[7] Although I have not suffered personally, it surprises me that anyone would identify with conventional truths that cause such enormous suffering. Indeed, I have found that most recent trans memoirists do not adhere to such conventionality and seem to favor a more personal, phenomenological account of their journey.[8]

Therapeutic approaches to trans identities have scarcely advanced since Harry Benjamin codified, through his extensive clinical work and in his 1966 book *The Transsexual Phenomenon*, the narrative of 'being born or trapped in the wrong body,' which surgery fully corrects. In this narrative, womanhood is achieved by terminating the transition in the complete rejection of any trace of male anatomy. Stone argues that this code has even impelled transgender people to present what is expected of them in order to receive medical and psychological support.

> It took a surprisingly long time—several years—for the researchers to realize that the reason the candidates' behavioral profiles matched Benjamin's so well was that the candidates, too, had read Benjamin's book, which was passed from hand to hand within the transsexual community, and they were only too happy to provide the behavior that led to acceptance for surgery. This sort of careful repositioning created interesting problems. Among them was the determination of the permissible range of expressions of physical sexuality. This was a large gray area in the candidates' self-presentations, because Benjamin's

subjects did not talk about any erotic sense of their own bodies. Consequently nobody else who came to the clinics did either. By textual authority, physical men who lived as women and who identified themselves as transsexuals, as opposed to transvestites for whom erotic penile sensation was permissible, could not experience penile pleasure. Into the 1980s there was not a single preoperative male-to-female for whom data was available who experienced genital sexual pleasure while living in the "gender of choice." The prohibition continued postoperatively in interestingly transmuted form, and remained so absolute that no postoperative transsexual would admit to experiencing sexual pleasure through masturbation either. *Full membership in the assigned gender was conferred by orgasm, real or faked, accomplished through heterosexual penetration.* (228) [Emphasis added].

A more sophisticated view takes into consideration the phenomenon of gender dysphoria or "gender dissonance" in Julia Serano's terms (2007: 1.1). In this case, one's physiological presentation does not match the inner identification. Serano parses gender dissonance in terms of a conscious and subconscious sex; she describes her first subconscious glimpses at the age of five or six, before social roles had consciously gotten fixed in her mind.

> I had dreams in which adults would tell me I was a girl; I would draw pictures of little boys with needles going into their penises, imagining that the medicine in the syringe would make the organ disappear; I had an unexplainable feeling that I was doing something wrong every time I walked into the boys' restroom at school; and whenever our class split into groups of boys and girls, I always had a sneaking suspicion that

at any moment someone might tap me on the shoulder and say, "Hey, what are you doing here? You're not a boy" (2007, ch.5).

This account suggests that gender dysphoria is not reducible to socialization. The discourse about dysphoria and its effects, seems to be divided into an affective aspect, and also a physical, even anatomical aspect (something that seems to suggest an essential source, but as we explored in chapter 3, we struggle to identify that source). Each memoiristic account of dysphoria is a little bit different, and this literature is likely to expand infinitely, the same way the subject of how love *feels* will never be exhausted.

I bring up gender dysphoria in order to underscore that conventional social roles are not the sole cause of an identity that seeks sex-confirmation surgery. Discourse about gender dysphoria involves both affective and physiological, even anatomical dimensions. Descriptions of how gender dissonance is experienced as a phenomenon fills numerous memoirs and first-person accounts. These subjective perspectives multiply as quickly as the instances. Moreover, the experiential dimension of being-other in identity from presentation could possibly inform many kinds of sexual and gender identity, not only trans ones.

However, a problem arises whenever discourse admits a codified interpretation of the body, which we observe in the earliest trans self-accounts of surgical metamorphosis. It is the enforcement of a body code that mires Trans-Exclusive Radical Feminist (TERF) ideology in the net of sophisticated hate-speech.

A bridge between the affective-phenomenological and the physical dimensions can be found in aesthetics, viewing the body as a spatial-temporal form that affects feelings.[9] We feel the form of our body when we are standing, sitting, or lying down; we feel more or less resistance, or friction; not just any form will do, if we are to find comfort. Our instrument must *feel* right, like a concert pianist sitting behind a meticulously tuned grand piano—everything must please, from the action to the tone. Athletes pay rigorous attention to their gear. The geometry of our bodies, sometimes down to the last few inches, impacts our experience of the world. This discursive frame might counter wrong-body narratives and open up clearer lines of communication between trans people and their lovers.[10]

Serano walks along the bridge of aesthetics between phenomenology and physiology. After a gradual transition from normative maleness through androgynous queerness to womanhood, Serano declares, "I eventually reached the conclusion that my female subconscious sex had nothing to do with gender roles, femininity, or sexual expression—it was about the personal relationship I had with my own body" (2007: 85). Serano invites her readers to imagine taking a million-dollar bet to live the rest of our lives as another gender. We might not jump at the chance, because we *do* have a deep-seated, dare I say, intrinsic sense of having a sex, being a gender. To repress the affective self-identity of our body would be catastrophically destabilizing. Confusion about whether that is me whom I see in the mirror is not sustainable. Serano takes this fact as evidence that one's subconscious identification with a particularly sexed body is unconditional.

> Let's face it: If cissexuals didn't have a subconscious sex, then sex reassignment would be far more common than it is. Women who wanted to succeed in the male-dominated business world would simply transition to male. Lesbians and gay men who were ashamed of their queerness would simply transition to the other sex. Gender studies grad students would transition for a few years to gather data for their theses. . . . Of course, such scenarios seem absolutely ridiculous to us. They are unfathomable because, on a

profound, subconscious level, we all understand that our physical sex is far more than a superficial shell we inhabit. For me, this is the most frustrating part about cissexuals who express confusion or disbelief as to why transsexuals choose to transition. They are unable to see that their disbelief stems directly from their own experience of feeling at home in the sex they were born into, their own gender concordance. (2007: 88).

I can appreciate this felt sense of being-at-home in a sexed body. Yet in the previously cited passage, Serano articulates a feeling that she was "doing something wrong" by appearing to inhabit a male body. The feeling of shame that can accompany dysphoria seems to me unfortunate; however, it pervades the literature.[11] *I too* am ashamed to be implicated in a social context that causes such unjustifiable shame or social pressure to match identity and physicality. I believe this context is produced by the cis hegemony's enforcement of codes that label bodies. I would contest the logic of the claim that a pre-social identity could feel the shame which social pressures create. Indeed, many feelings about the body seem like they are far more socially constructed than subconsciously absolute. For instance, why should we logically assume that a trans woman could feel longing to give birth, say, any more "deeply" or "truly" than a cis male father might fantasize, or a trans man realize?

Any person may well have a *pre-socialized dysphoria,* inchoate yet full of affect, not in accordance with labels, but with an aesthetic sense. One's body feels right, or it does not. I conjecture that trans experience often displays personal geometries that bracket or challenge the codes we habitually use to identify our bodies. To exemplify the tension, Serano writes (2007: 80): "If I were to say that I 'saw' myself as female, or 'knew' myself to be a girl, I would be denying the fact that I was consciously aware of my physical maleness at all times." We might continue to ask whether a feeling of "physical maleness" does not preload identity with too much socially coded information. What, if anything, makes the subconscious identity need to match the conscious presentation?

To Speak or Remain Silent?

Serano aptly warns about commenting on anyone else's gender or sexual identity, as it mostly reflects the critic's own gender entitlement.[12] Criticizing another's self-description dehumanizes them. "When we accuse someone of reinforcing the gender system, it is always a dehumanizing act—it allows us to ignore that person's experience or perspective because after all, they are colluding with our enemy" (Serano 2013: 136). Serano implores us to hold off criticizing others' identities because "challenging gender entitlement allows us to critique instances of sexism, while at the same time recognizing the fundamental heterogeneity of human sex, gender, and sexuality" (257). We do not need to criticize people's identities in order to criticize people's misconstruing of our own identities.

It is interesting to consider parallel cases of critique. For example, does freedom to live according to religious beliefs outweigh competing legal rights or civil decencies? Jehovah's Witnesses have been prosecuted for denying their children medical care.[13] Conservative Christians have been socially ostracized for refusing service to gay or lesbian customers.[14] What I suggest is that it is one thing to condone the low-hanging fruit of an anachronistic or violent religious practice; it is more difficult, and perhaps more beneficial, to sustain rigorous criticism of the underlying ideologies which undergirded those practices for so long. The most powerful engine of conservatism and the suffering it breeds—in my estimation—is the belief in eternal, inviolable essences that, however putatively natural, believers claim require vigilant protection against their "enemies" (Satan, change, chaos).

In my view, critique has a role to play when it comes to

the words people use to express themselves, which can combine into enveloping webs we don't want to be in; indeed, various kinds of sexism are often hiding in these webs of words and meanings. Serano demonstrates this kind of pointed, effective critique in *Whipping Girl* when she responds to a friend's question:

> He asked me, "Well, what if you found out that the trans woman you were attracted to still had a penis?"
>
> I laughed and replied that I am attracted to people, not to disembodied body parts. And I would be a selfish, ignorant, and unsatisfying lover if I believed that my partner's genitals existed primarily for my pleasure rather than her own. All that you ever need to know about genitals is that they are made up of flesh, blood, and millions of tiny, restless nerve endings—anything else that you read into them is mere hallucination, a product of your own over-active imagination. (Serano 2007, 279)

Serano will not be implicated in a web of meanings around a socially constructed standard of "proportional" geometries. Here is a fine example of well-formed criticism of another person's wrong-headed attitudes about gender and sex. Her friend's question threatened to involve her in a web of meanings she renounces—there is a sense that his attitude is faulty—so she skillfully redirects the conversation.

Serano notes the parallel of critiques of religious freedom to critiques of sexuality and gender. She contends that consensual participation in a given ritual or belief system is not a problem, but imposing one's beliefs onto others is. We must distinguish between, say, the burqa as a modest choice of garment and as a sign of oppression.

On the one hand, we each have a unique gender and sexual experience, where certain desires and expressions inexplicably resonate with us on a deep and profound level, while others do not. We should celebrate this heterogeneity. But there is also a "dark side" of gender—what I call *gender entitlement*—where we arrogantly project our worldview, our norms, our expectations and assumptions about sex, gender, and sexuality onto all other people, regardless of whether it resonates with them or not (Serano 2013: 242).

However, I think entitlement—and what, in some circumstances, we might call prejudice or discrimination—has roots deeper than projection. It could be argued that cissexual and cisgender entitlement runs deep in trans self-perceptions as well.[15] The supposedly proportional connection of words and bodies through such items as "sex" is at issue here. It would be nice for us all freely to articulate expressions that reflect what "resonate with us on a deep and profound level," but we must undertake self-criticism to guard against universalizing our preferences. Religious people can share or bear witness to their beliefs in relatable language, which does not presuppose assent to metaphysical assertions— generally the more personal and aesthetic their accounts, the less assailable they become to hostile critique. They also become less universalizable and reflect less entitlement and nonconsensual projection.

The *way* we articulate our convictions, the words we choose to express our identity, makes a difference. Words are not the pure reflections of our intention, to be sure; nor do they correlate unambiguously to the world. However, the spoken and written word puts our intentions into the world, and thereby makes itself accountable to others (readers, listeners, and bystanders) who share a world that is mediated by our words (Butler 2005). I would like to raise a flag of concern about Serano's claim that "when we accuse someone of reinforcing the gender system, it is always a dehumanizing act." It is perhaps dehumanizing to criticize a person for upholding a misguided, and *possibly* harmful, belief, although I readily concede that reinforcing the gender system is not an immediate threat as compared to some others trans people face. Yet much feminist and trans criticism of sexism does accuse people of reinforcing gender systems. A system enforcing stereotypes of real Men and real Women, with their "proportional" body geometries, can be toxic. Why shelter the system from justifiable critique?[16]

I have no doubt that trans people are constantly under investigation by discourse (including my book), and are consistently required to criticize violations of integrity, as victims of discrimination and prejudice. My only intent here is to bring into focus how transam identity contributes or not to the damage. I have personally experienced being derogatorily called a "faggot" by a trans woman for being sexually versatile. (I have observed a trans woman denigrated by trans women for lacking surgeries.) Such projections should not stand beyond criticism, but I think they are not incidental expressions, for they draw on a system that is toxic for *everyone*. It matters *how* we justify our beliefs and share our experiences.

My aim in this book is to justify my critique of the gendered and sexed norms that can stifle desires and expressions that resonate with me as a transam cis man. My method of justification is to show how conventional terms like "man" and "woman," "penis" and "vagina," "top" and "bottom" cannot transcend very limited conditions to become universal, eternal categories. Systems built on notions of real-man, real-woman, "passing," and compulsory roles are toxic, and deploying these terms uncritically should not be sheltered from criticism. I can attest that not everyone shares the reference points, which determine that, say, "man has penis therefore must top."

Better than current efforts to police gender entitlement, I think, are individual accounts of what resonates.[17] I also try to do it in this book, though it is not a memoir. The body is a place where we feel the impact of words, say, when they are fat shaming or ageist. That is not because of its *essence*, but because we are mired in *interpretation*—a learned, culturally sophisticated game of words. Interpreting the body is learned, and its unhealthy dynamics can be corrected. The human body is not putty, of course; but nor is it a rock. In her essay "Against Interpretation," Susan Sontag exhorts us to suspend our habit of interpreting works of art. In a world lived otherwise, she surmises, our lives too become works of art:

> Transparence is the highest, most liberating value in art—and in criticism—today. Transparence means experiencing the luminousness of the thing in itself, of the things being what they are. . . . The function of criticism should be to show *how it is what it is,* even *that it is what it is,* rather than what it means. . . . In place of a hermeneutics we need an erotics of art (Sontag: 23).

Those closest to us—our lovers and attachment figures—revolve around us in a close orbit; others circle further beyond. In this galaxy we all condition—both limit and generate—each other's bodily resonances. Sexuality may be the peak of embodied interdependence. The alternative to discourse based on endlessly interpreting fixed ideals is one of first-person *description*. Before turning to phenomenology as the alternative, I want to examine the interpretive codes of sexed and gendered bodies that cis people comfortably use, often to the exclusion of trans people, which may turn to hostility when the codes are endangered or threatened.

WORLDS OF INTERPRETATION
HOW WORDS HURT BODIES

The immoral and often sadistic treatment of trans women arises from the disruption of a mistaken epistemology that *interprets* the appearance of male and female bodies as housings for the inviolable sex and gender essences that culture uses to organize, and ultimately, misunderstand itself. The toxic cultural climate for trans and transamorous people is fueled by an epistemology of *interpretation* that we are not, in fact, obliged to perpetuate.

Loss and Murder

Between 2013 and 2015, at least fifty-three transgender women were murdered in the United States.[1] The figure does "not account for individuals whose deaths were not reported or investigated, nor for victims who were misgendered or not regarded as trans women in death."[2] As of September 2016, twenty-two more have been murdered.[3] More shattering numbers come from Brazil where, between 2008 and 2014, 604 transgender women were slain (again not accounting for unreported cases), with fifty-seven more killed in the first twenty-six days of 2016.[4] These disheartening statistics shed light on the disturbing reality that trans women are more likely than most of us to find themselves in precarious situations where violence escalates very quickly. While it is not possible to identify a common causal trigger in all of these cases, it is important to consider the similarities in cases where a woman's trans identity was clearly a factor.

The term "transphobia" is often used in connection with violence against trans people, but Thalia Mae Bettcher advises us to keep motives loosely defined. It is not necessarily or exclusively the transitioning aspect that motivates homicidal acts. As often as not, it seems, violence directed toward trans women is inseparable from issues of economic class, race, and misogyny.

> Such inseparabilities undermine the attempt to account for transphobia in a way that excludes or marginalizes considerations of sexism, racism, classism, ableism, and so forth. This consideration is important because it questions why certain instances of violence should be characterized as instances of transphobia (as opposed to racism or sexism) in the first place and what the underlying political agenda sustaining such characterization is (Bettcher 2014c: 251).

In the brutal 2002 murder of Gwen Araujo, where her trans identity was clearly a factor, Bettcher argues that the picture was complicated. Araujo was imperiled by transphobia; but she also was young, Latina, and female. Nevertheless, a singular threat facing Araujo and all trans women is the pervasive and persistent framing of trans women as "deceivers"—people who do not disclose "who they really are"—which to some is nothing but "men disguised as women" (Bettcher 2007:54). Bettcher, in examining the mechanisms through which this oppressive epistemological system functions, ascertains that most anti-trans hostility seems to occur when there is a rupture between external gender presentation (e.g., women's clothing) and the presumed genitals that the outer presentation would *seem* to announce. For most cis hetero men, there is the simple understanding that feminine accouterments function as synecdoche for a "real" woman's body. The prevailing episteme is lamentably one that strongly correlates clothing and genitalia. Sometimes what is left to the imagination, as it were, can surprise our expectations, if those expectations are dictated and reinforced by society.

How is a trans person not susceptible to appearing deceptive? Even were a trans woman (or man) to have bottom surgery, she (or he) might feel pressured to dissimulate about the past. The problem is with setting standards of sexuality—Real Manhood and Womanhood—that trans people (nor anyone else, as de Beauvoir points out[5]) cannot attain. Bettcher writes:

> Overall, I wish to stress that by making labels such as "deceiver" seem like inexplicable and bizarre stereotypes that are used against transpeople, or by simply claiming that transpeople are simply being ourselves, one overlooks some of the most important issues that confront transpeople. For because of the systematic representational alignment between gender presentation and sexed body, transpeople are never allowed to be ourselves in the first place insofar as we are fundamentally constructed as deceivers/pretenders. Nothing short of the elimination of this communicative relation will alter the deep social mechanism that prohibits transpeople from existing within dominant mainstream with any authenticity at all (Bettcher 2007: 55).

In other words, the language of "real" male and female bodies erases trans identity as such. In the case of Araujo, some legal commentators opined that while she did not deserve to be murdered, she had engaged in some degree of deception because she violated the social expectation that demands that outward presentation of gender announce an expected genital arrangement.[6] Rather than grapple with the implications of charging the victim with the offensive act of committing "deception," these commentators feel the need to develop legal protections so that "deception" not be admitted as grounds for murder. Bettcher notes the gross inadequacy of this "communicative relation" between cis people and trans people inasmuch as its definition of sexuality dictates the supposedly proper or appropriate correlation of inner and outer, attribute and essence. Bettcher doubts we will find simple ways to defuse violence against trans women, especially because transphobia does not seem separable from intersections of misogyny, racism, and other social ills.

> For insofar as the communicative function of female attire is determined by a model that embeds female bodies within a broader framework of naturalized rape, it is hard to see how gender presentation could lose its communicative force without also intervening in the very ways in which heterosexual sex and racialized bodies are fundamentally conceptualized. However, given the resiliency of racialized conceptions of the body, the centrality of genitals as sex determining, and the promotion of sexual objectification of women in the mainstream, it would also seem that transpeople will be deceivers/pretenders for a long time to come (59).

The Five Aggregates theory I reviewed in chapter 2 dismantles the "systematic representational alignment" of appearance and reality, attribute and essence, conventional and ultimate truths. The theory defuses the assumption that manifest traits have the "communicative function" to express a hidden substance. What Bettcher and Buddhist theories describe and criticize are epistemologies that thrive on *interpretation*.

According to Buddhist theories, we ordinarily form our identity by interpreting the existence of an essential self based upon a given set of conditional but nonvoluntary appearances, including physical form. The problem is not the appearances themselves; the problem is that we are fixated on identifying an inner self that putatively expresses its essence through outward appearance. Yet our appearances do not need the affirmation of an underlying essence in order to be authentic or true. The issue is not the arrangement of material conditions (HRT, surgery, etc. testify to the mutability of these conditions), but why we fixate on making sure these conditions manifest some real substance.

Bettcher takes a similar tack by pointing out an epistemological error that occurs when an appearance is interpreted to have an essential, inviolable entailment—for instance, wearing women's clothing *means* the person has a vagina; and when this heavily defended interpretation is challenged or refuted, people panic and react violently. Racism, transphobia, and sexism have this in common—an appearance is interpreted to have an essence that issues it, and any signal of a mismatch between them must be ignored or destroyed. In short, our epistemologies and metaphysics are pathological, and when their defenses are exposed, we may experience loss and suffering. Legend has it that when the Buddha taught of emptiness, his students became nauseated or fainted because they could not handle such a destabilization of their reference points.[7]

Loss, within the Buddhist taxonomy, falls under the category of "the suffering of change." For the perpetrator of trans violence, the loss they would seem to feel is a *symbolic* or interpretive kind. Their murderous intent is not motivated by self-defense or self-enrichment (such as in a robbery). They are motivated by a loss of self, a sense of humiliation or diminishment. If we listen to the perpetrators, they would have us believe they killed after seeing red; they lost themselves in a sexualized collapse of reason—the notorious "trans-panic" or "gay-panic" defenses are, unbelievably, admissible in courts to this day.[8]

The informal juridical category of "crimes of passion" has

excused the murders of innumerable women (and more than a few men and non-gendered people, as well).[9] They are one "deception" away from triggering cis male psychoses. One of Gwen Araujo's killers, who received oral sex from her, vomited upon learning of her trans identity.[10] This is precisely the protagonist's reaction in *The Crying Game* when he discovers the penis of his trans love interest. It is a familiar reaction people have upon experiencing tragic loss—the sudden death of a loved one, for example—but is there also a biological mechanism that jealously guards our fortresses of *meaning*? If so, can this natural instinct motivate, even justify, murder? The loss here that impels murder is hard to identify. Does the suspicion that they may "want" to have sex with a penis-having person threaten these men's "masculinity"? How does the loss of something as vague as sexual orientation—the violation of a metaphysical abstraction—trigger an animal's instinct for self-preservation? If we existentially attach to our heavily defended sexual identity, any suspicion or question about it is an existential threat.

Another victim of violence against a trans person was the Filipina Jennifer Laude who was strangled and drowned in a toilet by a U.S. Marine Corps private in 2014.[11] The perpetrator, Joseph Scott Pemberton, claimed in his defense to have killed this woman in order to fend off *his* rape by her. This young, trained military man "feared he would be raped" by a 120-pound Laude.[12] And yet Laude's reticence to disclose her trans identity before engaging in sex with a cis man was viewed as tantamount to rape or sexual assault, a position codified in forty-nine U.S. statutes.[13] The legal reasoning behind the obligation to disclose is not clear to me. The metaphysical one is obvious.

According to classical sexual ideals, when a man enters into sexualized contact with a woman, he must be on "top" and control the feminine object. The movements and language of the scene are scripted to interpret both bodies. We use words like "mount" and "penetrate" for stage directions. In actuality, the contact brings up all kinds of feelings and sensations, most beyond the pale of language's reach. So to relieve anxiety, a map is drawn, the land carved up and titled. Like the 1493 Treaty of Tordesillas fantastically distributed ownership of the imaginary world to Portugal and Spain, we mythically establish the sexual lot of Man and Woman. Sex achieves its dénouement when the Man achieves his goal of conquest. These codes and canons keep a lid on the vertiginously primal scene of sex.

When the trans person transgresses these boundaries, it appears that panic sets into an overblown interpretation, and the perpetrator spies a monstrous phallus. But their defense testimonies are shrouded in terms of "deception," "trap," and "rape," which name the violation of a "reasonably expected" heterosexuality as justification for murder. Again, destabilizing an interpretation issues in a feeling of loss. The too-common executions of trans women by cis men are tragic instances of this feeling coming up with no self-restraint or self-regard. However, the feeling also seems to overwhelm some men with less harmful consequence. Not only can violence be perpetrated but also intimacy can be damaged as a result of losing a precious script, map, or interpretation of sexuality. To make sense of this damage, I find myself conjecturing about thoughts of cis-het people I have met and observed.

Interlude: Reno, NV, 2015
A woman and her male friend are visiting town for the weekend, and they're back at their hotel casino bar for a couple of nightcaps. A middle-aged woman from the Midwest sits beside them and warms to their banter enough to join the conversation. A handsome young man comes to the bar and says hello to the older lady, whom he had met earlier. She introduces him to the pretty woman and her friend and they all take shots of tequila together. He asks her friend if they're a couple. "No, we're just friends." He looks happy and starts to flirt with her, loving her Spanish accent and dirty jokes. He plays baseball for the local minor league team.

Ten minutes later, his handsome friend joins the group. There is some competition between the two about who can impress the woman. But she knows where this is going. She has been in this scene countless times. She is thirty-nine, though everyone thinks she is much younger. She is the prettiest woman they've seen all night—probably a long time. Since she's with her friend, safe and getting ready to go to sleep, she changes the subject with a joke to one of the men and the Midwestern lady, something glib about her being transgender. The man stops flirting, indeed stops being a gentleman. He says something crass about her alleged penis. His friend, back from the bathroom, doesn't realize how everything has changed. He talks again to the pretty lady until his friend pulls him to the side, and they are gone.

I have personally witnessed this type of occurrence dozens of time.[14]

Many men would never consider resorting to violence, yet they find themselves attracted to a woman and then, upon learning she is trans, they suppress that initial attraction or sublimate it into a less disturbing (for the man) form. Their response to the "disclosure" of the woman's "deceit" is avoidance or aggression or both. For how can we un-see something we have seen? How can an initial impulse of attraction be negated retroactively? Erotic energies erupt into the real and can only be curtailed or mitigated by a counterinterpretation: "I was tricked." A widespread interpretation reads the trans person as a plunderer of cis-hetero sexual propriety. The trans person's very attractiveness to him is interpreted to mean a hetero man's identity is taken from him, and this interpretation impels his vigilant defense of his identity even to the disregard of others' feelings and decency. The media supports this facile interpretation, which shifts responsibility for any negative affect to the trans person.[15]

But how differently the scene above would unfold had the men accepted their confusion and not made it a catastrophe. Like putting a smooth piece of glass under a powerful microscope reveals a shockingly craggy terrain, the appearance of a trans body exposes the cracks and fissures in our precious, defended interpretations of sexual attraction and desire. Most people, but especially cis men, consider their sexual identity to be inscrutable and unassailable.

The anthropologist Clifford Geertz elaborates the process of becoming critically aware of hidden, bundled, entangled meanings—once interpretation subjects itself to interpreting. He starts by showing us that all interpretations take place in an interpretative setting or context, for "man is an animal suspended in webs of significance he himself has spun" (Geertz 5). He gives examples of how the critical eye sorts through a messy reality. First, he cites a thought experiment by the English philosopher Gilbert Ryle. Two hypothetical boys are observed to be rapidly contracting their eyelids. While any physical differences between the movements are imperceptible, there may be infinitely different meanings separating them. It could be that one of the boys has an involuntary twitch, perhaps nervousness or an eyelash; the other boy is *winking*.

> The winker is communicating and indeed communicating in a quite precise and special way: (1) deliberately, (2) to someone in particular, (3) to impart a particular message, (4) according to a socially established code, and (5) without cognizance of the rest of the company. As Ryle points out, the winker has done two things, contracted his eyelids and winked, while the twitcher has done only one, contracted his eyelids. Contracting your eyelids on purpose when there exists a public code in which so doing counts as a conspiratorial signal is winking. That's all there is to it: a speck of behavior, a fleck of culture, and voila!—a

gesture. That, however, is just the beginning. Suppose, he continues, there is a third boy, who, "to give malicious amusement to his cronies," parodies the first boy's wink, as amateurish, clumsy, obvious, and so on. He, of course, does this in the same way the second boy winked and the first twitched: by contracting his right eyelids. Only this boy is neither winking nor twitching, he is parodying someone else's, as he takes it, laughable, attempt at winking. Here, too, a socially established code exists (he will "wink" laboriously, over obviously, perhaps adding a grimace—the usual artifices of the clown); and so also does a message. . . . The point is that between what Ryle calls the "thin description" of what the rehearser (parodist, winker, twitcher . . .) is doing ("rapidly contracting his right eyelids") and the "thick description" of what he is doing ("practicing a burlesque of a friend faking a wink to deceive an innocent into thinking a conspiracy is in motion") lies the object of ethnography: a stratified hierarchy of meaningful structures in terms of which twitches, winks, fake-winks, parodies, rehearsals of parodies are produced, perceived, and interpreted, and without which they would not (not even the zero-form twitches, which, as a cultural category, are as much nonwinks as winks are nontwitches) in fact exist, no matter what anyone did or didn't do with his eyelids (Geertz 6-7).

Moreover, Geertz adds, "Ryle's example presents an image only too exact of the sort of piled-up structures of influence and implication through which an ethnographer is continually trying to pick his way." Transamorous relationships take on similar structures, in more or less exact images.

An information-item that most outside observers want to use for deciphering transam identity concerns genitalia[16] and

I have been regularly asked about my partners'. It seems vital information for most people to process their new exposure to a transgender person, to be able to place this person in familiar categories, even if those categories are now mixed up. If I have some confidence in the person's humanity and intelligence, I am usually frank, though sometimes I take the opportunity to suggest the reduction of an individual to genitalia is a dehumanizing act. Sometimes these conversations rapidly become invasive enough to broach whether I get penetrated, and I affirm my enjoyment of it as I watch them reconfigure their conceptual parameters for what defines a gay man, since not many people who know me see me that way, nor do I identify as such.

The problem here is one of *interpretation*. The questions I have fielded from my own friends provide enough information to make suitable interpretations of the appearance of transgender people in their social circle. My openness about enjoying bottoming, I have felt, is important for dislodging whatever notions they had about that particular kind of sexual behavior. They now might awkwardly think of me next time they hear a joke about "taking it up the ass"—it would not sound the same, the interpretive schematic had been complicated. And this can happen subtly.

Diana Tourjee's essay "The Straight Men Who Have Sex With Trans Women" tells the story of a man, Matt, who struggled in the past to be open about his attraction to trans women and became an advocate openly partnered with a trans woman. She writes,

> Matt briefly knew a guy who was dating a friend of Alicia's. "He was younger than me and he was seeing this girl. She was mostly a bottom, but then I guess she topped him one time, which is a stigma in and of itself. He said to me, 'Does that make me gay?' and I said, 'You know what? If it felt good and you're

making your partner happy, go for it. What the hell. Have fun, let it go.' I think hearing that from me made a difference in his life."[17]

Here Matt discourages the other man from interpreting sexuality with words whose meanings he did not consent to.

ALLIES INTERPRET, PEOPLE LIVE

Geertz's ethnography promotes interpreting human behaviors without fixing their meaning. It does not involve asking what metaphysical essence gets expressed. It asks instead about the "import" or the practical effect of the behavior (Geertz 10). A judging person may well insist that trans and transamorous people peddle in contradictions and lies, violations of natural law, confusion, chaos, and rebellion. But we expect better from those that know us. We prefer that interpretations not accede to predetermined entailments, that that they not take acts and bodies to be symbols indexed to metaphysical absolutes. We ask that they develop an interpretation that respects each act and person as elements of a "thick web of meanings," many of which are hazy and foreign to them. What precludes salubrious interpretation is simply "a lack of familiarity with the imaginative universe with which their acts are signs." The ability to understand is not about learning to speak a language, but about opening to another world of meaning. Geertz (316) quotes Wittgenstein, who says, "We learn this when we come into a strange country with entirely strange traditions; and, what is more, even given a mastery of the country's language. We do not *understand* the people. (And not because of not knowing what they are saying to themselves.)" We have learned how to say the words and what they literally mean, but we still need to get access to an entirely new "conceptual world" in order to converse with these people (24). To know what a blinking eye could possibly "mean," for example, we need to do more than learn a language; we need to swim in a culture.

As a result, in order to understand a phenomenon we do not need to share a firsthand experience, but we do need to have some share in the symbolic world that it makes sense in. Therefore, it does *not* require a living erotic connection—in fact, I will argue, *interpretation* has no place there—in order for a person to undertake *conscientious* interpretation. Geertz writes, "The essential vocation of interpretive anthropology is not to answer our deepest questions, but to make available to us answers that others, guarding other sheep in other valleys, have given" (30). A justifiable interpretation of unusual, unfamiliar bodies and behaviors must include a healthy dose of empathy. (Let us include bodies here, since we all know how the aesthetic, cultural, and ritual alterations of the body have multiplied to include tattoos and piercings of all possible variety.) Usually, though, people resort to their admissible frames of reference, like Christian idealism or psychoanalytic cynicism. Consequently, the cis-hetero man (or woman) who wishes to employ Geertz's intellectual open-mindedness in the face of unfamiliar sexes, genders, and behaviors needs first to set aside the many inherited prejudices which lead many to consider transgender people and their lovers as pathological, or even tragic.[18]

The human predilection is to index attributes to essences, which individual aggregations of attributes (i.e., persons) either conform to or deviate from. Measured against a standard of Real Men and Women, at best the trans woman is a sympathetic failure trying to achieve the impossible, an antihero who has abandoned the male citadel in search of a pure female form that is ontologically inaccessible to her. Thus, a woman's behavior, her dress, her style and manner are interpreted in a way that looks for how well they express the symbolic order. Is Womanhood expressing itself through this being as a conduit? Does it unfold through her as an instrument, or does it reach a dead end in the residue of the male she seems to be or have been? And her cis male lover is subject to the same interpretive gaze. Is he a Real Man? How can this coupling compare to a "normal" one? How is it that these two anomalous lovers define each other, and how does their coupling compare to "ours" (the hetero-cis-normative)?

This is a dangerous game to play, for it assumes a mystery, a gulf that can only be crossed indirectly. When it comes to eros, love, sex, and the body, interpretation will not do. Interpretations are better or worse, and they can change, improve or degrade. But it's still a world of gaps, mirrors, veils and encrypted messages. The worst interpreters of the body see the body and its parts as artifacts imbued with symbolic power, or "fetishes" in the narrow sense of the term. They see them as things with a meaning inhering in them, as things with a secret stamp corresponding to an eternal Idea.

The least suitable phenomenon to apply the Platonic Ideal is onto the body. As de Beauvoir notes, "The body is not a thing, it is a situation: it is our grasp on the world and the outline for our projects" (de Beauvoir 46). To be sure, interpretation has a role to play. Since the body is the site or medium of interface between self and others, it can be suspended in a world of meanings. But that suspension is not a prison sentence. We can imagine the interpretation is unfixed, the labels are nominal, and there are no essential truths. Our bodies comprise living documents and not strata of fossils.

De Beauvoir scarcely disputes the observable differences between sexes; she questions those differences' meaning or import. For instance, "When the physiological given (muscular inferiority) takes on meaning, this meaning immediately becomes dependent on a whole context; "weakness" is weakness only in light of the aims man sets for himself, the instruments at his disposal, and the laws he imposes. . . . Existential economic, and moral reference points are necessary to define the notion of weakness concretely" (46). Human beings swim in culture and our bodies are drenched with meanings, funneled through customs, channeled by norms. "It is not as a body but as a body subject to taboos and laws that the subject gains consciousness of and accomplishes himself" (47). In noticing differences between male and female sexes, the body is not identified in its own terms. (Needless to say, features differentiating bodies of "the same sex" are also observable: why else get hair implants or have breast augmentation surgery?) Rather, a distinctly formed identity—working, again, through culture—imparts meaning onto the biological differences between bodies.

Trans people are specific victims of our casually (and, occasionally, maliciously) indexed observable biological differences to fixed metaphysical and ethical absolutes. We can take an example from a mainstream conservative U.S. political journal, the *National Review*, which published *two* execrable articles by Kevin Williamson titled "Bradley Manning Is Not a Woman"[19] and "Laverne Cox Is Not a Woman."[20] Williamson's columns lament the proliferation of words to account for the diversity of human experience.[21] Williamson pines for a definitively established world of hard nouns that correspond directly to "real" things. A biologically determined sexed body determines gender, full stop. In particular, he asserts that nature affords two and only two possible combinations of chromosomes, one male and one female. Never mind that chromosomal analysis is a modern analytical instrument we ourselves constructed and does not index a god-given or natural kind. Never mind the material fact of intersex people who may have chromosomal characteristics that are inconsistent with their appearance, their attributes, or their identity.[22] As Williamson puts it misleadingly: "We have created a metaphysical entity—'identity'—in order to avoid talking about physical reality." This assumes fairly widespread delusions that "physical reality" is not a metaphysical construct and that "identity" is anything but a pragmatic articulation of being a self. It is a small step to the fatuous claim that "sex is a biological reality." The assumption that "sex" is less metaphysical an entity than identity has no merit.

Williamson bespeaks here a philosophical confusion worth clearing up. Metaphysical is *not* the opposite of physical. An abstract universal like "identity" has no concrete manifestation in the "physical" world, to be sure, but that does not render it de jure "metaphysical" in the pejorative sense Williamson gives it; it can have a certain practical validity as well (and certainly does for the self-designated "conservative" identity of Williamson). The definition of a *metaphysical* entity is one that is secured by an unassailable logic, irreducible and inaccessible to interpretation, a fixed reference point on the horizon of any (as yet incomplete) interpretation. For materialists, there are real basic entities—atoms and (negative) space. Any other word is a nominal label. Hence, there is nothing more real about "sex" than "identity"; even chromosomes are epiphenomenal. To endow such material data with ontological (Person A *is not* Identity Y) and moral significance (Person A *is* "delusional" for believing it), to interpret binary differentiation as a natural necessity, and to endow categorical essence with layer upon layer of interpretable meaning, *that* is the kind of pernicious metaphysical gymnastics Williams claims to object to, and it is, in my view, a grave misprision of gender and sexuality.

Thomas Laqueur has written a magnificent study tracing how the word *sex* has evolved radically in meaning over two millennia of Western history. Sex was a term used to make sense of an apparent binary structure of the species, a way to take inventory of differences between two general types of bodies. In early medicine, the main markers of difference were ovaries and testes, Fallopian tubes and spermatic ducts. For centuries, it was assumed that the ovaries were just an inversion of the testicles, and, corresponding to the misogynistic philosophies of Plato and Aristotle—as well as Paul's and Augustine's theologies of the body, where women are held culpable for original sin and punished for it by their inherited subordinate and dependent bodies—ancient science assumed that women were simply imperfect men, whose bodies were distorted for moral reasons.[23] (Common readings of the Bible's Book of Genesis chapters 2-3 legitimate this view.)

Kevin Williamson also turns the clock back to historical episodes in which questions of sex reared their head, noting the Roman Emperor Elagabalus, who desired to be a woman, and Nero, who tried to find a way to change the sex of a male slave he was in love with. In ancient times, sex and gender were thought to result from different intrinsic heats and metabolisms; the seat of sex was not the body, but the soul. Aristotle in *Politics* ranked man, woman, slave, and child, by the degree to which, in each category, the element of Reason prevails over lesser elements of appetite and emotions.[24] In this tidy schematic, physical differences convey a metaphysical hierarchy that grades the perfection of human life. More strikingly, still, Aristotle disembodies Man: "While the body is from the female, the soul is from the male."[25] Thus, it seems, all individual bodies aim to hit the mark of a universal Body—in the metaphysical Ideal or God's image—which is eternally male (and possibly not even a *physical* body). Unfortunately, more than half the world's human population falls short of the ideal image. Laqueur's analysis of ancient anatomical illustrations expose the remarkable degree to which doctors perceived the female anatomy, even under dissection, to have inverted male anatomy.[26]

Centuries' more scientific observation yielded more apparent anatomical differences (once menstrual blood, semen, and organs were understood more accurately) and led doctors to theorize the correlation between these anatomical differences and the subtler psychological and social differentiations that have been integral to Western civilization. This theorizing presumed the difference between Man and Woman was actually ontological.

> Thus the old model, in which man and women were arranged according to their degree of metaphysical perfection, their vital heat, along an axis whose telos was male, gave way to a new model of radical dimorphism, of biological divergence. An anatomy and

physiology of incommensurability replaced a metaphysics of hierarchy in the representation of woman in relation to man (5).

The ancient model of idealized sexual essence is, in some respects, more conducive to nuanced understandings of gender expression. Since *expressions* were reflections of an indwelling essence, it might acknowledge, or at least does not morally condemn, nonnormative sexual "kinds." Laqueur writes the following.

"You may obtain physiognomic indications of masculine and feminine," writes an ancient authority on interpreting the face and body, "from your subjects' glance, movement, and voice, and then, from among these signs, compare with another until you determine to your satisfaction which of the two sexes prevail." "Two Sexes" here refers not to the clear and distinct kind of being we might mean when we speak of opposite sexes, but rather two delicate, difficult-to-read shadings of one sex (53).

As we glean from Plato's frank discussions of pederasty[27] and the sexual promiscuities of Rome (see, for example, the erotic art in Pompeii and Herculaneum), the ancient world allowed for sexual differences between people to reflect indwelling essences, which fell *somewhere* along the spectrum of metaphysical perfection. These differences were not moral per se. Man and Woman are no different morally than water and ice are. They are simply different forms, or material instantiations, of the same One Form. However, differences were *also* interpreted by these ancients on a grading system that indexes the Male to the Rational, grants socially defined men (alone) access to the Good, and enjoins men to bring order and meaning into the world.

It is perhaps no surprise then that Christianity, through the inventiveness of Augustine of Hippo's conjoining ancient Greeks and the Bible, adopts this metaphysical framework where everything can be traced back to the God, the eternal first cause, the Father, the Male beyond the flesh. With the novel addition of instituting an ontological gap between God the Creator and the created world, moreover, the Christian worldview divides the sexes into *moral* kinds: fallen and saved, sinful and pure, etc. We see in Christianity—in total opposition to Greeks and Romans—the denigration of sexual pleasure, the advocacy of celibacy, virginity, and chastity, which take the body and its appetites to be essentially ungodly and . . . female. The sexed body thus becomes a battleground for moral codes, the most powerful tool for enforcing social roles. Their meanings are, of course, constantly shifting, but the binary reference points remain the consistent: Man versus Woman, Body versus Soul. Laqueur writes of the long Christian era: "Monks and knights, laity and clergy, infertile couples and prostitutes seeking abortion, confessors and theologians in myriad contexts, could manipulate it, as the facts of gender changed. It is a sign of modernity to ask for a single, consistent biology as the source and foundation of masculinity and femininity" (61).

The paradigm shift to modernity invigorated a cultural fervor to work out a unified theory of everything, where either matter or spirit reigns supreme. In the seventeenth century, René Descartes argued that only the mind is certainly real ("I think, therefore I am") whereas Francis Bacon determined that empirical facts alone are really certain. Regardless of their preferences, modern thinkers no less than premodern ones avidly sought the connection between phenomenal appearances in the world and their essential metaphysical correlates (even when those are called "natural laws"). After the Eighteenth-Century European Enlightenment, widespread secularization had loosened the fixation on a Platonic Ideal or Divine Image. That loosening fixation entailed an unsettling prospect—the prescribed social roles for Man and Woman lost their absolute, necessary grounding in previously upheld models of sexuality. Therefore, Laqueur writes, "When for many reasons, a preexisting transcendental order or time-immemorial custom became a less and less plausible justification for social relations, the battleground of gender roles shifted to nature, to biological sex" (152). Empirical data became a site of increasing scrutiny. Hitherto, the basis of sexual difference was ovary/ovum and testes/sperm. Twentieth-century science discovered hormones, and then settled on the chromosomal model of sexual difference. Regardless of empirical evidence and theoretical hypotheses, however, sexual differences are inevitably entwined with social and moral interpretations. As Laqueur puts it:

> We must not take for granted the terms in which science defined the new sexes. It claimed that the body provided a solid foundation, a causal locus, of the meaning of male or female. The trouble here lies not with the empirical truth or falsity of specific biological views, but with the *interpretive strategy itself.* Sexual difference no more followed from anatomy after the scientific revolution that it did in the world of one sex (163; added emphasis).

But this is just what Williamson and so many others imagine. He declares, "Sex is a biological feature that is present at the level of DNA."[28] As "true" as the genomic model sounds, that statement is dubious. Debates still rage about how to define sex even after the discovery of chromosomes. This is the subject of Sarah S. Richardson's book *Sex Itself.* Where Laqueur's study traces the long history of science's constant reinvention of sex before the age of DNA, Richardson focuses on the equally contentious status of sex after the riddle was purportedly solved. Just as with fluids, body parts, or hormones, "the X and Y chromosomes, little symbols of unbreachable sex dimorphism, come to anchor a conception of sex as a biologically fixed and unalterable binary" (Richardson 2). Conditional historic and subjective interpretation infuses this supposed anchor, much the way that cancer and HIV-AIDS are perceived symbolically, as Susan Sontag argues in *Illness as Metaphor*.[29] Sex, a complex entity that is more socio-linguistic than biological fact, is *interpreted* on the basis of collected data. Needless to say, as with any scientific inquiry, the data are incomplete. More, what do we even make of the data we have? Richardson cites several popular science textbooks where the author speaks of the Y chromosome as a miniature man, uncomplicated, pure activity, a stereotypical alpha-male that intentionally asserts itself in a microcosmic competition.[30] It is taken as the ultimate emblem for maleness, completing the circuit between the transcendent, infinite Male and the immanent physical detail that instantiates, or conveys, that truth in the world. Likewise, the X chromosome is caricaturized as mysterious, evasive, passive, and other stereotypical qualities attributed to the female sex or, more precisely, Woman.

Richardson refutes Williamson's projection. "There is nothing essential about the X and Y in relation to femaleness and maleness."[31] On top of raw data, layer upon layer of interpretive meanings are heaped, forcing social and moral significance onto the cellular level. The casual linkage between naturalness and social practices is a convenient way to dispel confusion surrounding sex and gender; but it is not therefore true. Williamson cites cases of forensic DNA testing that reveal the absolute male or female identity of criminal suspects or victims. But he does not wonder why the Olympic Athletic Committee abandoned chromosome testing in the 1990s because of the uncomfortable frequency of discrepancies between chromosomes and the lived sex of individual athletes, who had never identified as transgender or intersex until the test results.[32] Chromosome sex tests, with such heavy social ramifications, are problematic to scientists aware of the nuances of biological sex in general, and human sex in particular. In light of these complexities that are so willfully ignored by partisans of the inaccurate binary model, Richardson proposes a reconceptualization of biological sex that dispenses with the overestimation of X and Y chromosomes, one that attends to the details of sexual formation and abstains from *interpreting* them for social and moral significance.

> Classification of the particulars of nature into "kinds" is an integral part of scientific reasoning. However, what do we do with a kind that is at once one and two, like the genome of a sexual species? There are differences between properties of a population, properties of a pair, and properties of individuals. Thinking about "sex" requires paying attention to these differences. Sex is a relational property of individuals within a (sexual) population or species. . . . The sexes are not fixed and dichotomous subclasses within a population, but in dynamic interdependence and interrelation with one another. . . . Genetically, sex is a *dynamic dyadic kind*. . . . If sex is dyadic, one sex cannot be treated as an autonomous class, independent of the other. Sexes cannot be separated and compared globally as species and populations might. This would misrepresent the dynamics of sex as a biological kind. . . . Idealizing sexes as different classes or kinds, rather than continuous, interdependent, interacting classes, contributes to lazy sex difference claims. . . . Binaries invite dualistic, dichotomous thinking, so that it becomes difficult to think of a group of two without subsuming one into the other, ranking them, implying polarity of complementarity, or posing them as opposites (198).

Richardson's approach to defining sex does not erase an undeniable difference, yet she does refrain from hypostatizing that difference and turning each mark of difference into a repository for social and metaphysical meanings. While chromosomes have been observed to be markers of *dyadic kinds* within a species, their exact role remains unclear. Indeed, "sexual dimorphism may be reliably transmitted without a genotopic dimorphism such as sex chromosomes."[33]

This picture highlights the incredible diversity of individuals that are the products of such unlikely comings together of different conditions and differential processes. Williamson and others grasp at whatever possible metaphysical bedrock they can for their ideals. Even if they did acknowledge that the riddle is not perfectly solved, they assume it is a matter of time before the exact combination of genes, hormones, and other factors is revealed. And in the current absence of this knowledge, we can be content in the conviction of its advent. With the abstract term *sex,* we seem to encode metaphysical categories. But in reality sex is imagined "all the way down."[34] The "dualistic, dichotomous thinking" in Williamson's articles are dissected by Richardson.

> We should examine whether the term "sex chromosome" remains apt. Consider the parallels between the term "sex chromosome" and the contested term "sex hormone." Scientists and gender analysts alike have criticized the term "sex hormone" for distorting biological reasoning about sex and gender difference. The terms "sex hormone," "male hormone," and "female hormone" mislead by obscuring the roles of this class of hormones in biochemical processes other than sex-specific and reproductive ones. As a result of these critiques, endocrinologists have moved away from this terminology and now instead use the terms "steroidal hormones" or "gonadal hormones" for this class of molecules. The term "sex chromosome" leads to similar distortions in our understanding of

the functional organization of the human genome. As discussed above, the symmetry ascribed to the X and Y because of their status as the sex chromosomes has oversubscribed their importance to the determination of sexually dimorphic and reproduction-related traits while undersubscribing other factors (206).

The search for two real human sexes—Male and Female—has been misguided. Not so long ago, racial difference was held to be ontologically valid, just as we think of sex now; and the quest for truth about race was finally abandoned by science conclusively. Richardson sums it up:

> Biological conceptions of human sex difference have changed over time, shifting with the privileged theories, methods, and interests of the dominant biomedical research program. Reproductive organs, blood color and density, skeletal morphology, brain size and lateralization, and hormones have each been claimed as the "essence" of human sex difference. For much of the twentieth century, genes and sex hormones held a friendly détente, genes responsible for throwing the initial switch to determine sex, hormones for all the complexities and riches of sex difference. Today, genomics is increasingly the preferred language for explaining and describing sex and gender differences.

Steven Jay Gould's *The Mismeasure of Man* (1996) traces two centuries of attempts to establish a biological basis for the argument that non-whites are less intelligent than whites. Gould shows how each attempt to do so was discredited, then replaced a few years later by another research program looking for racial differences in new physical substrates, with new technologies and with a new set of terminology. The history of attempts to establish the biological essence of sex difference and the physical and mental inferiority of woman follows a similar trajectory (225).

This is again a good place to bring up the importance of critique. While racial "biological" science based in racist social codes endured for a long time, in the end it perished under the weight of the scientific evidence and inquiry.

Even if we had been able to trace a biological mechanism that differentiates people from different demographics, what would we find? When people stopped *interpreting* biological data under the influence of an idealistic bias, that bias lost steam and is slowly staggering its way out of public discourse. With sex also, it would be more healthy and helpful to break the assumption, bias and projection that fills the world where our bodies and words conjoin toxic meanings, and the multiplicity of individuals living in the world languish in stifled and stymied positions. In the next chapter, I make the final case for us to proceed, in sexuality and gender at least, against interpretation.

AGAINST INTERPRETATION

LIBERATING BODIES
FROM RESTRICTIVE LANGUAGES

Susan Sontag opens her short and masterful essay, *Against Interpretation*, by saying that "the earliest *experience* of art must have been that it was incantatory, magical; art was an instrument of ritual (cf. The paintings in the caves at Lascaux, Altamira, Niaux, La Pasiega, etc.)" (1). I follow the method I laid out earlier for the aesthetics of eros to its logical conclusion. Undoubtedly, experiences of sexuality were incantatory as well. But the time arrived when those bodies were no longer taken for themselves and came to stand for something else.[1] We learned that in us dwelled some kind of purpose, and that purpose achieved its realization through proper, proportional deployment of resources (attributes or features), and through the appropriate combination of sexed bodies acting as ciphers for another power or reality (e.g., the gods, God, evolution). Once symbolic interpretation sets in, lovers no longer simply touch and taste, envelope and fill each other. The wonder and delight slip away, replaced by codes of conduct and systems of meaning. Sontag concludes, "None of us can ever retrieve that innocence before all theory when art knew no need to justify itself, when one did not ask of a work of art what it said because one knew (or thought one knew) what it did. From now to the end of consciousness, we are stuck with the task of defending art" (2). Sontag's history of art's origin is speculative, yet the experience of wonder and delight that converts into a symbolic order is widely discussed in aesthetic theory (beginning at least with Immanuel Kant and Romanticism).

As with art, I submit, erotic encounters also got mired in interpretations that wove around bodies and behaviors as humans, detached from touch and taste, sought reasons, raised defenses, and quarreled. With regard to sex, I admit, we are entering slippery terrain, more loaded with ethical quandaries than art. Because admitting some distance or social space between sexual partners would also commendably introduce considerations in the sexual realm, such as the differentiation of physical force and mutual pleasure. However, the interpretation too quickly takes on a life of its own, quite separate from bodies adored and behaviors enjoyed. Sontag laments how experiencing art is abandoned in or submerged under the rush to interpret. While art is not sui generis and lives in its own context, with the advent of interpretation, its possible horizons and dimensions are foreclosed, channeled into limited options. As Sontag put it, "We have an obligation to overthrow any means of defending and justifying art which becomes particularly obtuse or onerous or insensitive to contemporary needs and practices" (2). Indeed, how much more of an obligation do we have to overthrow any means of defending and justifying bodies and behaviors that have become particularly obtuse, onerous, or insensitive.

To be sure, our bodies and what we do with our bodies fall under the gaze of interpreters. Interpretations may not annihilate us, but they do curtail. The interpreter "without actually erasing or rewriting the text, is altering it. But he can't admit to doing this. He claims to be only making it intelligible, by disclosing its true meaning" (Sontag 3). This comment returns us to Bettcher's notion of "reality enforcement."[2] It cannot be that you are *really* that mysterious, feeling, desiring being there in the flesh. You aren't really what you feel you are. In the TV series *Sense8*, the trans character Nomi Marks is threatened with a lobotomy because she is not really seen as who she says she is. She is Michael, her mother insists with the support of powerful reality police. This is, unfortunately, the essence of too many psychological views of trans people. Who you are now must emerge logically from who you were in the past, and the sexed body is born that way; what you do now, your habitual behaviors, are the unfolding of an essence that that is unalterable and, more important, enforceable.

*

We seek alternatives to interpretation, because interpretation, in its basic anxiety and dissatisfaction, too often misses the mark of—and even damages—experience (as Sontag argues of art, and I argue of eros). Yet, it is the heart of criticism and judgment. Harnessed with methodical procedures, interpretation can both yield enlivening insights and reign in unsettling differences. How many of us have failed in a relationship because someone said something we could not let go of? Or suffered mistrust of a loved one because a text message was left unreturned? What do we make of the coworker's declining our invitation to lunch? There must, we assume, be a *reason* for everything; and it is incumbent upon us to find that reason and respond to it accordingly. Things cannot happen in ways we do not understand. Everything is interpretable.

Sontag points out the dangers of thinking this way. Where interpretation transgresses its limits as an intellectual tool that dusts off new facets of old gems, it takes on a life of its own and inserts itself into our social and ethical world as a hostile enforcer of a predetermined reality. Nothing should happen by chance. Sontag was investigating illness and found in it a metaphor fostered insidiously by so many in society—from guilt-tripping doctors and self-involved purveyors of gossips. The unscientific assumption shared by all too many people is that an ill person must have given herself a tumor through psychosomatic self-harm, as though "one is responsible for one's disease."[3]

The assumption hidden in our metaphors of illness is that the body is coded, and its code is the expression of desire and will. One's cancer cannot be a mutation, a biological accident with plenty of its own logic to make it understandable as a burden—without adding the moral interpretations of weakness and failure. The ill body is not a text requiring interpretation. All bodies, whatever their condition, are a site of experience, a modality of sensation. Reading illness as a code embodying (hidden) intent is uncaring nonsense.

The sexed and, especially, sexual body is not an ill body, nor is it any more so a text. The sexual body outstrips every interpretation of it, such that any interpretation feels in some way like a stretch. The experience of sexuality, or the erotic, involves an uncontainable and irrepressible charge of energy. No doubt, the energy can and should get curtailed when it becomes "particularly obtuse or onerous or insensitive to contemporary needs and practices." If the excessive charge is altogether lacking, the experience as such is altered, if not erased, as in the experience of art. I wish to address the excessive curtailment of erotic energy as a problem for trans people and the transam.

Much of our contemporary discourse about eroticism views desire as the expression of a lack. That lack or deficiency is corrected by the sexual act. The putative drive to procreate, to reproduce the species is a most common interpretation we apply to, and enforce codes for, sexual behavior. In this frame, sexuality carries with it metaphors of the soul mate or one's "better half."[4] The female is the receptacle as the man is the penetrator. What each lacks, the other provides. One without the other remains incomplete. Each part is required to make sexuality whole. This entire interpretative framework relies on the essentialist assumptions that I criticized in chapter 2. It assumes that sexual being conforms to normative categories, or it is a perversion. Much of what passes for admissible discourse about trans people, such as that they are "deceivers" or "delusional," is almost precisely what was (and still is) projected onto homosexuality, onto BDSM, even onto bearing children out of wedlock (taxation in the U.S. enforces this code by rewarding marriage). As individuals we are all subjected to the category we were born into. Man has vaginal intercourse with Woman *for a reason*; every other act is either strange or an abomination. Of course, tossed onto such a neat graph, many of us are outliers; but, according to Idealist assumptions, it is not the responsibility of the normal to accept the deviant. Therefore, erotic ambiguity, nuance, and subtlety are only the machinations of the confused, and likely pathological, human being.

This is a bleak picture of sex. It is one thing to objectify, to dehumanize the erotic object (and that is something everyone must be vigilant to avoid; interpretation and critique have its limited function, to be sure) but it is rather tragic and inhumane to deprive the erotic subject of its rich dimensionality, confining it to a normative structure. I am saddened that people would choose to limit themselves in this way; but I am angered to feel these people project their folly onto others who are not so captured by an imaginary, Idealist norm.

Here I find it helpful to read Thalia Mae Bettcher, who subverts this normative sexual dualism with an elegant addition. Bettcher proposes a tripartite, self-reflexive dynamic of the erotic experience. "Sexual orientation is not merely determined by stable gendered 'object preference,' but also by stable 'preference of gendered self'" (Bettcher 2014: 607). This concise proposition flies in the face of idealist thinking, which, in its binary code of sexed bodies, cannot apprehend a "preference of gendered self." What is this novel category? "Sexual attraction to a person possesses an internal, constitutive structure that includes the eroticized self as an element. . . . Erotic content is not exhausted by the source of attraction (the person to whom one is attracted). To be erotically interested in something (to be aroused by it) is not necessarily to be attracted to it" (606). It is important to notice how sexuality is a dialectical or dialogical experience because it does not only involve the attractor and the attracted but also attractiveness as an event or a process. "Sexual attraction admits of an interactive structure in which eroticized experience of self and other are mirrored through eroticized interactions" (611). The bipolar attractions of fixed gendered selves primed for intercourse turn out to be static, its conclusions foregone. To give an example, I may find myself in a sexualized situation with an erotic object, a genuine beauty, say, yet nothing in this polarity ensures that the sexual situation becomes erotic; my erotic object may end up talking too much, or I may feel nervous or a cold coming on; or perhaps I find *myself* unattractive. Erotic experience is not inevitable simply because two mutually attracted bodies meet; a multitude of conditions must be met, as well.

Bettcher elaborates the multifaceted features of the sexual dynamic, which is not determined exclusively by the erotic object. "An erotic interest is a 'source of attraction' when it plays a certain structural role in 'the complex of attraction'" (Bettcher 2014: 611). She illustrates this complex with the example of how a predominantly gay man might summon pleasure when receiving fellatio from a woman even though she is not, for him, intrinsically a "source of attraction." He achieves pleasure by populating "the complex of attraction" with sufficient conditions—for instance through the fantasy of imagining the warm mouth of his fellator to be that of his male paramour.

It seems likely that many "exclusive" couples' erotic experiences also figure into a "complex" that is larger than any given "source." Pornography, role-playing, and BDSM practices are some ways to feed or nurture the erotic encounter. Moreover, it is not simply that the source of attraction may need supplementing or replacing in a complex of attraction. We also must invite the erotic attraction into ourselves as well—including our very own bodies. Since this may sound, rhetorically, a bit like the idealist and theological discourses I have inveighed against, let me clarify and simplify the point. For the moment to be erotic, we have to *feel* erotic in our bodies. Innumerable factors contribute to the feeling. We don't usually feel erotic when we are sick, or when we notice the person before us does not see what we would like them to see, that they are projecting onto us, attracted to something we do not believe ourselves to be, or when we feel objectified. It can happen that the situation ruins the mood for us, takes away our intimate contact with our very own bodies. There is no source of attraction per se.

Attraction happens in context.[5] It has a history; it has been conditioned by multiple factors. Our parents, our community, our society influence any complex of attraction. The body itself is an accretion of conditions. The swarm of matter pours and tumbles, and our body is passed under the spigot and becomes the vessel of a tiny draught. The object of our desire then is not like a rich target in an open field. It is more like an image we catch a glimpse of behind the veil of many images, some attractive and others not. This is why the erotic moment is not a linear act like filling a hungry belly, but rather an unlikely, unforgettable arrangement of myriad factors that somehow in the moment unleashed a potential born uniquely of that arrangement.

The erotic experience is not one of exchange or, worse, acquisition, but of unfolding play; Bettcher uses the familiar metaphors of boundary ordering and boundary crossing to describe it.

> Physical intimacy primarily involves *sensory access to bodies*. It also implicates specific activities which require various types of sensory access to bodies as a part of the activity structure. For example, fellatio requires sensory access to a penis through the medium of a mouth and sensory access to a mouth through a penis ... Intimacy, however, does not merely involve

increased sensory access. Rather, it requires *interpersonal boundaries* traversed in cases of mutuality and transgressed in cases of abuse ... In order to *traverse* a boundary, a *movement* from one stage (of intimacy or non-intimacy) to another more intimate stage is necessary. Consequently, interpersonal boundaries are vaguely ordered sequentially so as to allow for socially recognized degrees of closeness. Different kinds of sensory access "occur earlier that others" (a woman's breasts are touched before her genitals) as do sexual activities (kissing comes before heterosexual intercourse). Indeed nakedness, I have argued elsewhere, is a mode of self-presentation that is every bit as socially constituted as the clothed mode of self-presentation. In particular, it is constituted through these interpersonal boundaries regulating visual access where the ordering of boundaries gives the body a moral structure. As a result, attraction has a temporal aspect. What is missing, in this view, is not merely sensory access to a body part, but to an *intimate* (private) body part that is part of a larger ordering of boundaries (14).

In this "erotic structuralism," the subject and object of attraction, attracted and attractor, are not lined up like phalanxes on a battlefield. Rather, they are orbiting each other in an emergent galaxy, or a masquerade ball.

Sex-differentiated bodies have distinct "boundary structures" applied to them, constituting nakedness differently. In effect, there are two main types of nakedness—female and male. One difference is that the former has a tiered structure whereas the latter does not (i.e., female chests have a moral significance). Since to be attracted *to* somebody is to be aroused *by* the traversal of structured boundaries, different types of sexual attraction can be distinguished on the basis of which structures of nakedness are in the erotic context (16).

I differ slightly here, since I believe the male anus is also laden with culturally fabricated moral strictures and taboo.[6] Still, Bettcher is correct to suggest our bodies are multilayered, entangled in a mesh of references, meanings, and feelings, which mutually condition—reinforcing or rejecting—each other.

Bodies in physical intimacy draw close, unfold and uncover themselves and each other. The heights of passion, when subject and object seem to melt away in total abandon, require the orchestration of innumerable parts, which amount to their paradoxically simultaneous unification and annihilation.[7] It helps to feel *how* our partner desires us and to have a sense of *why*. Bettcher explains the situation for her hypothetical lovers, Germaine and Sheena:

> Contrary to the view that Germaine is aroused by the "female physique," then, Germaine is aroused by the female physique as *implicated and structured within a system of ordered boundaries governing sensory access to it*. . . . Sheena's own visually-accessed body is part of her erotic content (even though she is not attracted to her own body). Moreover, Sheena's erotic self is given by the same boundary structure (to which Germaine is attracted). That is, a specific feature of her eroticization of the increasing transversal of boundaries between self and other is that her own boundaries be structured in a particular way, namely female. For example, her arousal at Germaine visually accessing her breasts requires precisely that her own body have a female boundary structure (16).

Differently sexed bodies have differently structured boundaries, and these deserve a careful treatment that does not assume any metaphysical necessity. The "female boundary structure" functions nominally as a label for a bundle of social, psychological, and biological factors. It is not a static metaphysical reference point; even less an elusive essence possessed only by a "Real Woman."

Boundary structures are relevant to our discussion of transcis sexual relations because they can give rise to anxiety and may involve a sense of dysphoria. The peril of speaking of *male* and *female* boundary structures resembles the peril of speaking about art pointed out by Sontag. By *interpreting* boundary structures, we may see our lover's body as the perceptible vessel of a hidden content.

The alternative to interpretation that fixes a boundary structure is imagination. Where interpretation decodes appearances in order to master reality, imagination opens up an appearance to entertain multiple novel realities. Bettcher looks at what sexual fantasizing does. For instance, a man who is attracted strictly to other men can use fantasy to eroticize the feeling of a woman's mouth on his penis, even though she is, in herself, not a source of attraction for him; in the same complex, the woman could be attracted to other women and imagine herself orally stimulating a lifelike strap-on dildo.

> [The process of imagination is] one of various complex activities and fantasies in which some trans people engage in order to re-code their bodies to lessen body dysphoria, while allowing certain body parts to become part of a sexual encounter. For example, if a trans woman (with a "penis") is receiving oral sex, it is possible for her and her partner to erotically re-understand the activity as a form of cunnilingus rather than fellation, perhaps by eroticizing a component of her genitals as a "clit." Practices of this type

involve two features. First, "re-coding" can invoke the re-imagined body part being taken up into the erotic context. Second, that there is this erotic uptake does not undermine the capacity of the trans person to be sexually attracted to a partner (11).

Bettcher elaborates on the process of recoding, adumbrating what she calls the possibility of "interpretive intimacy," where the trans person and their lover can traverse erotic-bodily boundaries and achieve a satisfying erotic interaction by creatively re-interpreting each other's bodies and behaviors. In this model, to interpret does not mean to access a real truth, as it does in the essentialist model criticized by Sontag. There is no static truth to be uncovered in the bodies or behaviors of trans or transamorous people. Interpretation, rather, would be an art of opening up to imaginary possibilities. Instead of excavating a fossil of reality, it reinvents the erotic in the given reality (the being into which we are thrown), and allows us to build and inhabit ever better realities. In the conventional binary sex model, we are *really* one sex or another, and our sexual activities are defined, made sense of (i.e., interpreted) according to those defining categories. This attitude is at the heart of the "wrong body" model in transgender discourse.

> In the wrong body model, transsexuality is construed as a misalignment between gender identity and sexed body where the identity is innate and determines one's *real* sex. It's on the basis of this identity that one affirms that one has always *really* belonged to a particular sex where the morphological body is viewed as "wrong" and in need of surgical alteration. In the transgender model, trans people experience oppression and violence because they challenge the view that there exist two nontraversible mutually exclusive categories in which all individuals belong. Their

so-called "beyond the binary" status is seen as the source of conflict and hostility (2013: 53).

There are, of course, physiologically differentiable marks of the binary sexed/gendered being—the penis and the vagina. Yet Bettcher notes how these marks or signs in trans people's sexuality do not undermine but, rather, make explicit the places that body parts fit and the roles they take on.

This can obviously lead to challenges when negotiating sexual activity (particularly when sexual scripts centralize those body parts). Ironically, it is precisely such situations that provide trans people with the opportunity to reinterpret their bodies and to do so in an intersubjective way (at the very least, since they are the very few occasions in which these parts are involved). What gives sexual interaction such a powerful capacity for reinterpretation is, in part, the fact that in a sexual context, fantasy and role play are permitted to an extent that is not normally acceptable in mundane public interactions. That is, within a sexual context, there is an element of playfulness that opens the doors of possibility, paying less attention to the constraints of social reality (55).

Bettcher's point here about eroticism presenting an opportunity for the playful adventure of human being to unfold is not an uncommon one to make. Among others, Michel Onfray in his *A Hedonist Manifesto* echoes the point, and universalizes its value beyond the trans discourse. Onfray explains how, in the West, a predetermined reality was strictly enforced. Specifically, these were tightly bound with procreation. Recently in the West, the decoupling of procreation and the erotic has encouraged new interpretations of sexual pleasure and activity.

Changing customs, along with changes in science, have given us a chance to truly master reproduction with the aid of contraception. While the Church publicly denounces it, contraception allows for a revolutionary disassociation. It can give us sexuality for pleasure, without fear of engendering something to be experienced as a punishment. The libido is free to find playful combinations, not just those that are obligatorily procreative (Onfray 2015: 62).

More than ever, we human beings have a chance to reinterpret sexual bodies and the sexual behaviors that take place in and between them. For example, the sex-positive movement assures cis-hetero partners that no consensual activity in particular is perverted or undermines a partnership. For cis-hetero lovers, the stakes are relatively low. As Bettcher points out, trans people's every action—from self-presentation to the erotic deployment of their genitalia—is monitored by under the directives of "reality enforcement." Reinterpretation involves "offering positive narrative interpretations that run against mainstream invalidation" (2014: 59).

Bettcher (2013: 611), citing C. Jacob Hale (1997), points out a common way trans people begin to recode their bodies and redefine the activities their bodies take part in by altering the labels that compose their sexual narratives. For example, a trans woman may refer to her anus as a pussy—a simple verbal substitution that can contribute to a more creatively self-validating sexual experience. Here the trans woman confirms her participation in the sexual narrative as a woman, inasmuch as sex-policing forces tell us that women have vaginas. Some trans women exclude body parts from sexualized attention. It is my personal experience that excluding the penis from sexual activity, while under the impression that it represents a marker too close to being Male, is perhaps a valuable resource to the trans person, but it also raises questions. As a transam sexual partner, I have felt like I was being asked to be a party to reality-enforcement, and like a functionary in a project I did not believe in. To my mind, the exclusionary interpretation seemed to rely on the metaphysical assumptions Sontag criticizes. I got a weird feeling that I was expected to be in communication with Man and Manhood, who were supposed to direct me like a marionette. I couldn't be what she wanted and couldn't be myself; and she probably felt the same way.

The method of verbal reinterpretation destabilizes meanings. The genitals can be whatever they are physiologically, and not be fixed to any definitively sexed and gendered body. We can rewire our circuits of attraction. The penis that is labeled a clitoris, for instance, is not the ideogram of manhood. In my experience this play has allowed the *whole* body to participate, and therefore, the whole self, even if some parts were assigned unconventional names. In erotic situations guided by the verbal method, bodies do not need to follow a conceptual plan or ritual. Bettcher explains the magic that verbal imagination brings.

> One might understand one's gender identity (as a woman, say) to accord perfectly with one's body (including a penis). That is, by recognizing trans women as women, one could understand one's penis as entirely congruent with one's womanhood. This would involve a reconfiguration of genitals (as they are related to the concept of a woman) and also the very concept of woman itself. This last move opens up notable possibilities. For example, it could make sense for a trans woman to engage in active penetrative intercourse with her penis without this activity invalidating her trans womanhood. The social meaning of the activity and its relation to womanhood will have to be reinterpreted (55).

Bettcher adds that trans bodies and behaviors must contend with the experience of misidentifying with certain parts and acts. But she rightly suggests that it arises from bad, that is, ill-fitting interpretations.

> Trans bodily dysphoria is an interpretive affair that pertains to social meanings attributed to body parts rather than body parts taken as entirely independent of social meaning. While this might suggest that trans people would be better off trying to alter the meaning of their bodies outright, it is also important (as Hale notes) to recognize that there are individual limits for trans people on how much reinterpretation is psychologically possible (56).

Our empathy for trans lovers recognizes their experiencing dysphoria. But Bettcher does not explain *why* certain people might therefore assume that "there may be no choice but to either forego sex altogether, have sex in such a way that excludes the body part as much as possible from the situation, or have sex that is to some degree unpleasant" (56). I would conjecture that since dysphoria is "an interpretive affair," a matter of variable meanings that are socially and culturally constructed, it has history. History can be traced, and its effects can be changed.

C. Jacob Hale writes about his own personal impasse in expressing all the sexual behaviors expected of him as a [trans] man.

> Some ftms[8] who used to be leatherdykes may have found, as I did, that there were limits to our abilities to reconstitute the sexualized social spaces of our bodies. Some of these limits are constituted personally in that we cannot ourselves reconfigure the social meanings of certain bodily zones, and others may be externally imposed in that we cannot manage to communicate

our attempts at idiosyncratic rechartings in ways that others are able and willing to read (Hale 231).

Crucially, Hale considers interpretations to be flexible. And the final sentence highlights the need for opening pathways of communication between trans people, who are internally embarking on "idiosyncratic reachartings," and those who "read" or interpret them through social or erotic interactions. It seems to me these pathways must be far away from the cluttered thoroughfares of interpretive schematics. The most compelling alternative, I think, is that of descriptive phenomenology stripped of fixed, referential meanings.

The meanings of signs are historically conditioned, I have claimed in this chapter. When we learn to interpret this or that sign, someone is—more precisely, many people are—telling us that it represents this or that idea or principle or truth. We have all been to the same general school of our civilization. If our anxieties and others' intolerances are not natural but learned, they can be unlearned. As Hale points out, as individuals, we are unlikely to vanquish the horde of meanings that impinge on the freedom to be who we are and would like to be. As individuals we sometimes want to throw up our hands and play *their* game as best we can.

Sometimes all we have the energy for is to take part of us out of play because the judges would penalize us for using it. This is clear in the reasonable desire for many trans people to live without fully disclosing their identities to everyone freely. But it also applies to transams who seek resolution to their struggles in assimilation. Or, with a little more energy, we can change the words of the game and lighten our shoulders from the metaphysical burden the old words carried. But in the fullest sexuality, we cannot leave our bodies to words. Just as Sontag argues that *interpretation* will always stand in the way of aesthetic experience, and that "in place of hermeneutics we need an erotics of art" (10), so too, so much more so, do we need a naked, nondiscursive erotics of amorous, mutually attractive, consensually touching bodies.

There may be many ways to do it, but there exist specific methods for sloughing off the calcifications of verbal and symbolic meanings that cling to us like barnacles. There are ways of peeling back, paring down, or suspending the layers of interpretation that cloud a more naked world that could shine. *This very world* before our eyes, the world that offers you the beloved flesh, the warm and steamy world that licks between your thighs, a world that requires no mystical entrée, one that we've been cut off from for most of our lives. Noble traditions take this world as their goal and have charted compelling paths to get there. In the next chapter, I look at trans and transam identities through the nakedness of their bodies.

THE NAKED WORLD

MERLEAU-PONTY'S PHENOMENOLOGY OF THE BODY WITHOUT INTERPRETATION

In the rich tradition of Tibetan meditation theory, a famous expression compares the mind in successful meditation to a child who has entered a temple for the first time. Although somewhat culturally specific, the image of a Tibetan temple is meant to convey a sense of wonder at the sight of vivid colors and vibrant sounds, the rich smell of incense, the high ceilings, and the smooth silks of hanging banners. We can imagine the first time we attended a crowded event, the first time we went to a mountaintop. Unburdened by a dictionary full of terms, we did not flit from one part of the spectacle to another making associations; we did not read faces, the way people danced or sang, or the things they wore for significance. Moments unfolded before us, mouth-breathing in awe. Cousins had holes in their shoes, neighbors brought coolers full of food and drink, and brother brought his friends. There was no embarrassment for uncle out of work, no envy of the neighbor's nice car, and no judgment on dates and company, what kind of family they came from, what they talked about alone. We were there to play, to let the sights and smells and tastes wash over us and leave us wet in their wake. We grew a little, and we heard reasons why cousins' shoes were worn out, we heard reasons why mom her brother don't get along, we heard our older sister crying and fighting with our parents.

Frustration, money, divorce, depression, and goals—new terms in our mouths and new guests in our heads. Sex education, the mechanics of coitus, pregnancy, STDs, friends and family asking who we like, popularity contests, movies, romance, porn, fantasy, expectation, execution, consequences, reputation, friends, our first sex—disappointment, bliss, bragging, secrets, discussion, feelings, and anticipation. How did it go? What did they think? What now? Attached, jealous, self-conscious.

Gone, for most of us, are our wide eyes.

For the young queer lover, hiding shame, secrecy, hope, and lack of hope, this is the erotic landscape. Flooded by inputs from every angle, we are not left to play. We attune ourselves to the thoughts of others and investigate the extrinsic meaning of what we are doing, wearing, who we are fucking, how we are fucking them.

In the last chapter, we saw Thalia Mae Bettcher's analysis of how hard it is for trans lovers to know a truly naked body—a body denuded of social entailments, a body bare of signposts and the reference points of cis-normativity. The allure of coitus, the pressure to have *the* surgery, the hypostatization of real men and real women, the habits of culture perpetuated by the grinding wheels of prescribed roles and behaviors. The banishment of body parts, making enemies with whole erogenous zones, the cascade of significance that follows some kind of licking or sucking or penetration.

For the transamorous person, it's the gay or bi question, the entailments, and identity becoming squiggly. . . .

Jonathan Kemp explores the galaxy of meanings attached to certain combinations of the body, in particular, the taboo of the penetrated male. Kemp observes, "The penetrated male body represents reason's other; that there is a certain madness attendant upon excessive pleasure which links with passivity, submission and femininity" (20). Each term is pregnant with meanings produced and propagated through popular discourse where it is "as if, for the male, to experience submission . . . is always already coterminous with getting fucked—an expression which in itself indicates the slippage between the sexual and the metaphorical registers of speech" (74).

But it is not only speech. The wide-eyed moment doesn't last, the child in the temple is asked where he came from, why he is there, where he is going. The wet, naked moment of (at least) two glowing, eroticized bodies dries up and they become a text to be read, rewritten, and shelved as objects carrying out some social objective. Our partner's flesh stops swelling and warming under our touch and our eyes squint to read it as a map, its contours flattened into lines and signs. We ask an expert to tell us what each act and object signifies at a higher level. Thousands of tomes of academic writing navigate and expand the morass of sexual symbology that bloats our lives. Psychoanalytic industries thrive in this fecund and fertile environment. A transamorous cis man falls in lust or love with a trans woman and opens his body to her as she does to him. The days and weeks are a blur, confusion.

If he happens to be wealthy enough to have access to a professional sexologist and their shop of narratives, or if he seeks clarification through reading, he may hear something like the following, which may confuse him even more.

> Within the Lacanian economy of sexual differentiation, of course, the role of master signifier is filled by the phallus, that absent leader to which we are all expected to defer in order to make sense of and register wishing the symbolic order. For a man, therefore, to rebel against the master signifier is to lose the privileges obtained though being a "member" of the group marked "male," a membership contingent upon having the phallus. To abdicate the phallus is thus to submit to a masochism marked by a loss of

masculinity, through castration; to have one's membership rescinded: one becomes a symbolic "woman." To submit to that leader, however, is no less masochistic, for it places the male subject in a threateningly homosexual and, within such an economy, feminizing subject position. The male body must submit to the Phallus in order to become male. Paradoxically, that is, the male body must be penetrable in order to enter a symbolic order which will subsequently disavow such penetrability, providing that body with a phallus that acts as a guarantee against it, for within the symbolic order only those without the phallus (i.e., "women") can be penetrated (Kemp 64).

These insights give a faithful rendition of *why* our transamorous man might feel anxious. Here are the normative meanings. The threat he feels for loving a trans woman is real because of the way he has tampered with privilege, with patriarchal roles, the way he has loosened a few screws in the scaffold. But he reads the heavy terms and has to ask himself if they apply to him; how well do they apply to him? Does he have the wool over his eyes? His wet, naked moment, his open body, the fullness she lent to him, are hollowed out now, spread in an analytic array, their erotic density put through a sorter. While intellectually sound, erotic-meaning analysis burdens the lover—especially the newly self-aware transam, or the transitioning trans person—with the weight of centuries of ideological baggage. Their bodies are not free to play; they are not let to be their own beings sailing a course toward self-constitution.

If intellectual, and especially academic, discourse tends to generate evermore lines in the net of these entrapping significations, it does not mean we turn our backs on them completely. Intellectual work is not identical to conceptual proliferation, the elaboration of meanings, and interpretation. We have seen how the work of interpretation drains the erotic of its intimacy, its fleetingness, and its openness. But philosophical methods do exist that go the other way, that recognize the parade of lights (meanings and interpretations) dancing on the surface of life, and lets them dance, and returns attention to their naked ground. In Western literature, it is hard to find a book that articulates this return more exhaustively than the *Phenomenology of Perception* by Maurice Merleau-Ponty, who describes his approach as "a philosophy for which the world is always 'already there' before reflection begins—as an inalienable presence; and all its efforts are concentrated upon re-achieving a direct and primitive contact with the world, and endowing that contact with philosophical status" (Merleau-Ponty vii).

That inalienable presence is our right, as lovers, as people alive and laughing and crying. It is who we are before we read ourselves with and against the meanings dumped on us by our caregivers and society, it is our body, our self, hanging there as it does among feeling, perception, volition, and consciousness—undeniable yet only present in the strange moment when analysis is suspended.

We suspect and we even know that we don't need to be told what we are, what our bodies might mean, what we represent when we hug and kiss and love and fuck. We pour other people's readings of us out in our best moments; we let them drain and soak into the ground, which they can't intimidate, where they do no harm. We enjoy those moments of a bright and present self and body, full only of its own spontaneous presence, not the labels and chains cast on it from all the surrounding interpreting gazes. But we have to go outside, we have to go to work, to a family dinner, to a party, or a public bathroom; and then we're deflated, paradoxically, as others fill us up and turn us into symbols, as we are taken for nodes in some vast social fabric. We can't run and hide from the gazes. There's no refuge, no "safe space." There's no way to go back in time and undo the many streams of meaning flooding into and over us; their history has massive weight and momentum. The break, the gap, is found in the ongoing moment; it is found in the brief suspension of interpretations' reach and in bracketing all the meanings we are so familiar with and weary of.

If this sounds abstract, it isn't. It can amount to a flat refusal to accept and propagate habitual social and personal sensibilities and attitudes; to stop interpreting ours and others' bodies according to canonical sets of meanings; to cease being and acting with a constant eye on the symbolic entailments of our being and actions. For example, not long ago I had a conversation with a trans friend who was talking about the next steps she would take in her transition. Her priority was to train to feminize her voice, and she was contemplating future surgeries. She said she had recently caught herself looking in the mirror and it occurred to her that her body "looked like it should have a vagina." I asked, "According to whose codes?" She ended up talking about social and historical forces that implanted her with that impulse to interpret her body according to what it *should have* as its symbolic, synecdochal organ. At least for the duration of that conversation, she loved her body as it was. But the body takes its own directions; no one can entirely determine them in advance. Some actions are more permanent than others.

In Merleau-Ponty's philosophy, "To return to things themselves is to return to that world which precedes knowledge, of which knowledge always speaks, and in relation to which every scientific schematization is an abstract and derivative sign language, as is geography in relation to the countryside in which we have learnt beforehand what a forest, a prairie or a river is" (ix). As with many great philosophers, Merleau-Ponty could not have anticipated how useful this approach could be for twenty-first-century trans and transamorous people who intimately know, and have every right to name the forests, prairies, and rivers of their embodied lives; who are entitled some freedom from the abstract and derivative sign language that tries to appropriate their erotic bodies and expressions and assumes there is an essence to them that can be decoded through some cis-normative key and tries to explain where they came from and what their place is—*what they mean.*[1] An interpretation based on the presumption that the world *ought* to be the way we commonly, or historically, experience takes things and people in the world as interpretable texts and symbols holding an old and sacred code within them. Everything is a walking Idea conceived by some inaccessible mind and maker. However, Merleau-Ponty discovers, "looking for the world's essence is not looking for what it is as an idea once it has been reduced to a theme of discourse; it is looking for what it is as a fact for us, before any thematization" (xv)—the world as a fact for us, as well as our own facticity, naked and awake, before the veil and obscuration of *meaning* takes hold.

The lover experiences the satisfaction of his (in the case of the transam cis-male) actuality in the presence of his lover, when his mind and body forget about the snares set up around them by the public gaze. And he lets that presence be snatched away, or he clutches desperately to it as it is torn from him. When Julia Serano describes the experience of the trans child,[2] it sounds like the child would like to dwell in this facticity—an awareness of presence—before school and puberty and family turn them into a theme of discourse, a hero or a villain, a supplicant for paternalistic accommodations of meaning. The child feels herself adequate and full, until encounters with others turn the tables, instill doubt, and make her leap over hurdles of meanings. To live is to encounter, but whether these encounters are hard or soft depends on so many things, especially the gaze of another. Merleau-Ponty continues: "The phenomenal world is not pure being, but the sense which is revealed where other paths of my various experiences intersect, and also where my own and other people's intersect and engage each other like gears" (xx). Gears that power engines of meanings, which rain out like sparks, forging hard and rigid units; or gears that move more gentle warp and woof, weaving a finer tapestry. "We witness every minute the miracle of related experiences, and yet nobody knows better than we do how this miracle is worked, for we are ourselves this network of relationships" (xx).

We are situated in a network of relationships, and these relationships inform how much we hurt or feel at peace. These relationships will be colored by the lenses other people look through, by the tone and energy they bring in. Nobody knows better than we do how to make our body and mind sing—that is, until everything in the world convinces us we do not know best, until we're instructed in the implications of our erotic feelings and the true symbolic nature of our bodies or parts of our bodies. The paths of our various experiences, the ones we feel when no one is looking, not even ourselves, those paths that are our very ground, get muddied and dusty when they intersect with the gigantic, anonymous thoroughfares of meaning. We spin and can't find our way; our trails are swallowed into the uniformity of the canonical veneer slathered on the world. The naked world we touch only sometimes in art, in bed, in conversation, among friends.

> When we come back to phenomena we find, as a basic layer of experience, a whole already pregnant with an irreducible meaning: not sensations with gaps between them, into which memories may be supposed to slip, but the features, the layout of a landscape of a world, in spontaneous accord with the intentions of the moment, as with earlier experience . . . To perceive is not to experience a host of impressions accompanied by memories capable of clinching them; it is to see, standing forth from a cluster of data, an immanent significance without which no appeal to memory is possible (Merleau-Ponty 21).

Outside of the erotic, our bodies have grooves of meaning imprinted on them—meanings constructed through often-painful histories. In many spheres—those of family, school, work, and politics—the world is too sharp and rushing, the consequences of passivity are too great to suspend the discursive, connection-making, synthetic mind. In social realms, we try to forget our naked bodies.

But the body *is* the site where history carves its memory. Ta-Nehisi Coates reminds us in his book *Between the World and Me* that the black body is at issue in racism—not the mystical and invisible black soul, but the visible and physically burdened black body. Politically, the black body cannot escape the significance of its appearance. It is impossible and disingenuous to try to suspend the black body's inexorable symbolic reality, the way that in the U.S. it is like a mirror that reflects our origins in violence and violation. Like a mirror, the body itself has no intrinsic, mystical content, but it cannot help but reflect what passes before it. It does not want to reflect pain and wounds, but trauma cannot simply be wished away; it hangs in the atmosphere and weighs on different bodies unequally.

We may note a similar issue for trans bodies. It may be no coincidence that many of the most influential trans public figures of late are trans women of color. Coates highlights the black body's basic lack of security in America, the way the police and systems of incarceration consume black bodies like fuel, where statements like "I could have you arrested" really mean "I could take your body away from you." This insecurity, the chaos of having your body besieged by so many people around you, is compounded for trans women of color, whose bodies are taken from them at an alarming rate.[3] The heart of activism is to remind us of this, to shine harsh light onto the reality of people whose bodies have come to mean they are sites of painful experience—simply because of the symbolic history of trans and black bodies. Politically, socially, publicly, the meaning carried on the backs of bodies should remain of central concern.

Unlike social and political space, there are nonetheless ways in which the erotic space *can* be a refuge.[4] For Eros to breathe, there has to be air. The cacophony of voices, observations, and interpretations has to settle into more mellifluous tones. In the intimate sphere remains one of the few places it is safe, necessary, and nondestructive to suspend the signifying mind.

The term preferred by phenomenology to describe this suspension of the signifying mind is "bracketing." In math, when you bracket a term in an equation, you set it aside; it remains there, it has not been *removed,* but it is set out of play temporarily. The erotic suspension of interpretation and signification is not, must not be, a denial—political and social meanings are not wiped away or repudiated in these moments. They will flood back soon enough when the tenuous erotic moment is encroached upon and rattled back into the social realm of interpretation. The bracketed domain can be a place where all that matters is the body's presence, not its social and historical symbolism, not even its sexed or gendered identities.[5] It can be a place where all that matters is the chemistry between you, not the social and political consequences of bodies interacting; a place to be with a lover truly without judgment. "To perceive in the full sense of the word (as the antithesis of imagination) is not to judge, it is to apprehend an immanent sense in the sensible before judgment begins" (Merleau-Ponty 35). There is enough sense in your lover's body, and your own, right there, resting in its own place.

We bracket the political, social, and historical in the erotic moment, but this bracketing has profound implications on those realms. Far from denying the reality of historical and political significance, their temporary suspension exposes them for what they are—historical conditions and social constructions. However, whatever is conditioned and constructed is also mutable and revisable. The erotic moment provides a gap in the onward-rushing stream of time, a place of new possibilities, a refuge for a kind of nondiscursive imagination. Merleau-Ponty writes, "When I contemplate an object with the sole intention of watching it exist and unfold its riches before my eyes, then it ceases to be an allusion to a general type, and I become aware that each perception, and merely that of sights which I am discovering for the first time, reenacts on its own account the birth of intelligence and has some element of creative genius in it" (43). Through this kind of non-interpretive contemplation, we gain conviction that the meanings carried by our bodies and entailed by our acts are not intrinsic, natural, or eternal. These moments in which we take in each other's riches unfold and exchange mutual glances and caresses in unrestricted play are not *naïve*.

The erotic moment is a time to train in the better world we may wish for ourselves in a given time and space. It is a surreal time, during which painful weights can be set down, yet we feel it as vividly as we feel anything else—even more vividly, perhaps. It is another space, in which surfaces play with each other and *also* touch deep parts of our soul. For the transamorous man, immersion in the phenomenology of the erotic moment and taking its lessons into all the moments outside of the erotic, he can learn to articulate his body his own way, to reclaim it from the discourse that has always told him what his body means and what the bodies of his lovers mean. Calvin Thomas writes about what a big problem it has been for men, and all the more for transamorous men whose sexualities clash with the canonical symbolic order:

> Men's refusal to think, speak, and write their bodies helps to make history rotten in the first place. The refusal to tell the truth about the male body is the precondition not only for the effacement of those bodies in the existing representation—that is, in the truth according to the phallus—but also for the continuing displacement of the question of the body only an actuality coded as feminine. Nothing could be more repetitive. The longer male theorists forestall attempting to tell the truth or say something specific

about the male body, the longer we continue to bear witness to the truth of the phallic law and to reproduce ourselves as the agents of patriarchal domination (Thomas 36–37).

In addition, Thomas highlights the nearly complete elision of *anality* from any positive articulation of straight male sexuality.[6] Thomas asks the question, "What if we reversed the normative process by which the anal ... [as Freud says] remains the symbol of everything that is to be repudiated and excluded from life" (Thomas 68)?

The transam man might contribute to filling in some of the lacunae of male sexuality by grappling with the polysemous nature of holes and organs. Whether or not he bottoms, his sexuality is linked to the anal, and if *he* does not articulate this anality, those inexperienced will. Even if he is with a trans woman who has had a vaginoplasty, cis interpreters of their relationship may slip, even against their will, into discursive thoughts about her anatomical and sexual history, imagining, with difficulty, that her sexuality must have undergone a mysterious anal-to-vaginal transmigration. What, they might wonder, does this *mean* about her partner? Yet the hetero male voice is silent about the body. It has preferred to talk about the ideas that guide their love lives ("She is a woman. I am a straight man.").[7] Merleau-Ponty point out that:

> For Freud himself the sexual is not the genital, sexual life is not a mere effect of the processes having their seat in the genital organs, the libido is not an instinct, or an activity directed naturally toward definite ends, it is the general power, which the psychosomatic subject enjoys, of taking root in different settings, of establishing himself through different experiences, of gaining structures of conduct (158).

Salamon provides an astute commentary on this element of Merleau-Ponty's approach.

> An insistence that phenomenological experiences of the body and the subject are individual rather than categorical situates the subject differently, temporally and socially. In terms of social organization, this insistence on particularity frustrates categorical summary; it means that neither sexual embodiment nor situatedness nor expression can be predicted by membership in any particular category of gender or sex. The implications of this disarticulation are more profound than the comparatively clearer decoupling of sexual identity (male or female), gendered identity (man, woman, femme, butch, or trans), and sexuality (lesbian, gay, bisexual, or heterosexual). Nor is this an articulation of the now familiar enough notion that feminine desire is by its nature unlocatable, diffuse, ambiguous . . . I am interested in arguing that an embodied response to desire is, through its radical particularity, unpredictable and impossible to map onto the morphology of the body. A woman's experience of sexuality may be tightly and intensely focused on a particular region of the body or it may be distributed throughout the body. So too, might a man's. That is: we have zones of intensely erotic pleasure, but the relation between a body part and its erotogenic or sexual function is perhaps one of lightly tethered consonance rather than a rigidly shackled indexical mapping. And while a sexual physiognomy might be "outlined" by the erotogenic zones, the body's morphology is not determinative of the location or behavior of those zones, but rather, is determined *by* them. Merleau-Ponty is insisting that sexuality is not located in the genitals, nor even in one specific erotogenic

zone, but rather in one's intentionality toward the other and toward the world (Salamon 49-50).

The phenomenological erotic moment is not a vague abstraction. Accessing the erotic moment, what academic phenomenology calls the *phenomenological reduction*, allows us to wipe all the dust off the mirror, to see it bright and bare. But it is never static; all the things of the world never really disappear; they are simply put out of play; they are allowed to rest and they let us rest for a moment. But there will arise restlessness. There is always more to express, display, reach, and combine. And the body can do it. "The body is the vehicle of being in the world, and having a body is, for a loving creature, to be intervolved in a definite environment, to identify oneself with certain projects and be continually committed to them" (Merleau-Ponty 82).

There is meaning in the satisfaction of bodily resonance, and there may be times the body must be tuned and adjusted, through surgery or whatever else, to achieve it. "Sometimes, finally, the meaning aimed at cannot be achieved by the body's natural means; it must then build itself an instrument, and it projects thereby around itself a cultural world" (Merleau-Ponty 146). Like Prometheus stealing the fire from the gods to enrich humanity's resources for forging its own destiny, we try to seize the freedom we need to own our own bodies, to make them the finest instruments of our own musical tunes.[8]

Yet the struggle, and the loss, is real. We can only stay absorbed in the erotic moment—the phenomenological reduction—for a limited time. Most of our life is lived in the aftermath, the wake of those epiphanies where the meanings imposed by others are immobilized and rendered transparent. But those moments can inform the way we navigate the cultural world; they lend clarity to our demands of society and chip away at its policies and its nonconsensual touch and gaze.

In the context of transamory, by taking the refusal to code as the path, by making policy of the moratorium on interpreting the body and the things the body does with other bodies in an erotic moment, a space opens for us to breathe when the natural flood of signifying besets us again. When a systematic erosion of habitual interpretations of our bodies and sexual acts has taken place, new and better codes will have the conditions to arise and take root. Here are the apt words of Merleau-Ponty.

> [The body] is not a collection of particles, each one remaining in itself, nor a network of processes defined once and for all—it is not where it is, nor what it is—since we see it secreting in itself a "significance" which comes to it from nowhere, projecting that significance upon its material surrounding, and communicating it to other embodied subjects . . . The body must in the last analysis become the thought or intention that it signifies for us (Merleau-Ponty 197).

No defined network, no predictable cluster, but rather an ever-shifting cluster that constantly turns and sloughs itself off and again takes in the material of the world and holds it as a piece of itself. "My body is the fabric into which all objects are woven, and it is, at least in relation to the perceived world the general instrument of my comprehension . . . It is my body which gives significance not only to the natural object, but also to cultural objects like words" (Merleau-Ponty 235).

It is especially important, I believe, for transamorous people and their lovers not to let this fabric be stolen by those who would weave ugly meanings into it. If it is an instrument, we must tune it to play our music, not anybody else's. Merleau-Ponty's interrogation of the body does not diverge radically from the insights of the Five Aggregates. He explores the self's conventional presence somewhere there suspended in, linked to, but not identical with the body. Salamon comments, "The body itself is, finally, a mixture or amalgam of substance and ideal located somewhere between objectively quantifiable materiality and its phantasmatic extensions into the world" (64-65). Merleau-Ponty perhaps does a better job than the Buddhist discourse of bringing the physical body—the aggregate of form—to life, of highlighting its inextricability from the other four, more ideal aggregates. In particular, he gives a vibrant account of the role of volition—or at least one powerful kind of volition, desire—in orienting the body in the storm of reality, where infinite relations and meanings are possible.

The transamorous lover, in the light and shadow of Merleau-Ponty's gleaming ambiguity, can soften their gaze and shut down the meaning-factory of interpretation that takes their body and their lover's body as symbols, that takes the erotic combination of them to be some kind of equation that yields a certain significance. The phenomenological method—even understood as simply a suspension of discursive thinking—furnishes gleaming shears for cutting away the ropes that tether us to immature and oppressive sexual attitudes.

A PERSONAL TRANSAM SEXUALITY

MY BODY, MY WORDS

Previous chapters have emphasized the openness and variety of trans and transamorous embodiment and sexuality. The phenomenological method provides a space that every individual may travel through and explore on their way to self-realization, which necessarily includes the body and the way the body relates to the world. But once some of this work has been done, once we are aware of what magnetizes our bodily energies and why, and what means of expenditure best satisfy our bodies, what to do next? If our discoveries are unexpected, if they distinguish us from our peers according to their own expressions, should we keep them to ourselves, so as not to trouble the water, or because we are embarrassed? Or is there benefit in sharing that part of ourselves, as uncomfortable as it may be?

As already mentioned, trans issues have long been conflated with hypersexuality and deviance, so there is danger in foregrounding sexographies that may contain elements of hypersexuality and deviance. For this reason, I excluded most sexual details from chapter 1, emphasizing there other equally (or more) important obstacles to having fulfilling relationships, including a lack of shared intellectual, spiritual interests, and similar experiences. But if those sexographies are nonetheless thoughtful and self-critical, is it beneficial to *suppress* them in order to make trans and transamorous sexualities virtually indistinguishable from "wholesome" heteronormativity? In our discussions of Sandy Stone's work, we have seen that at least a generation's worth of trans sexographies were based on willful obfuscation. Trans subjects were compelled to misrepresent their own sexualities for pragmatic reasons, or they were obligated to comply with and conform to the canons of the medical and psychological institutions they needed access to. Whole generations of trans women, especially, were conditioned to despise their anatomy and interpret their organs and actions in prescribed ways. There was little freedom to explore, let alone share the findings of one's explorations.

Sexual activity may be the murkiest of all topics in transam relations. Not because there is some incommunicable secret, but because every person's sexuality is unique and becomes doubly so when combined with another person's unique sexuality. Therefore, no account of transam sexuality is at all representative; it is only a map of personal desires and proclivities. Some of these desires will be shared by others, and some will not. Never do they find their exact twin. Therefore, it is tempting to remain mute on the topic, to keep what is personal private. But this strategy has only fed confusion and assumptions about transam sexualities. I can only speak of my own sexuality, representative of no one. I offer my account—a confession— only as a sample of sexual diversity, and I hope that others will be encouraged to embrace their own stories and share them with others.

One reason this is important is to counter the assumptions about transam sexualities that come from all quarters. I personally have experienced some of the effects of the phenomenon of compliance that Stone observes. Some of my trans women lovers have seemed invested in hierarchical, essentialist notions of Real Man and Real Woman, and what sex acts are valid and invalid between these two types of idealized body. We don't hear many accounts of transams at all, especially not first-person accounts. Even in private conversations, transamorous men tend to be quite coy about their desires and impressions, first trying to gauge their interlocutor's prejudices and adjust their confessions to mitigate harsh judgments.

In chapter 1, I discussed the issue of the "tranny chaser" versus the "authentic transam," observing how the former is often marked by an avowed affinity for trans people, while the latter is marked by innocence about trans identities. When this trope is presented so frequently, it misrepresents transam relations on a number of levels, and it sets up a harmful ideal that arguably alienates transams and trans people.[1] For one thing, this trope elevates the ideal of the "passable" trans woman, presenting the ideal as a gateway to love and happiness. The trope also feeds the myth of trans woman as deceiver "trapping" just the right man who is so self-secure that he lets her off the hook for her trickery. Those are issues for trans women to debate, as Julia Serano and Thalia Mae Bettcher have done in ways I have found incredibly helpful.

In this final chapter, I will look at how the tropes of the "trap" and "chaser" uphold the rigid sex and gender norms that cause so much suffering to begin with. In my opinion, they tend to glorify the "innocent transam" and can, in turn, disparage the man with an acknowledged yen for trans women. Yes, despicable "chasers" do exist, but the vilification of openly transamorous men—especially those who have had several trans partners—will I think be an obstacle for everyone involved in transam relations, and for anyone outside them to understand them better. Undoubtedly some trans people *and* some transam people continue to have an affinity for binary heteronormativity, but the rest of us would do well to discuss our sexualities more openly with each other, to refine the map of the sexual landscapes that surround us.

I, for one, write from the perspective of a cis man who is avowedly what is called a vers-bottom. This means that I do, under the right circumstances, enjoy being the more active or penetrating member in a sexual encounter, but under most circumstances I prefer the other way around. I prefer to be penetrated, or to have my partner direct the proceedings. The exact ratio will vary from person to person depending on their own desires and needs, and what desires they evoke in me, making me versatile. But as a reference point, my most satisfying long-term relationship, sexually at least, was one in which my trans female partner was the active (top) member by far most of the time. By and large, and if I were forced to choose only one, I would prefer the bottom role, and a bottom role of receptive penetration.

A feature of my sexuality, which affects every relationship and even informs who I court or flirt with, is that it is more anal than phallic. I truly derive more pleasure and satisfaction from anal stimulation than from traditional phallic ejaculation, that *sine qua non* of male sexuality. While desires do evolve, this has been my preference for many years, and at this stage in my life it seems to me wise to embrace and emphasize this aspect of my sexuality rather than put myself in more situations where I am expected to repress or sublimate it. The reasons for this are probably impossibly complex, and were I ashamed or troubled by my sexual lot, I could employ a therapist for years to mollify my anxieties. I will explore some of the reasons below, but at the risk of oversimplification, I believe it comes down to a matter of psycho-physical constitution—the constitution of one's particular swarm of aggregates, those shifting sands that make us what we are. With these unique constitutions come unique "complexes of attraction." My constitution has yielded a sexual anality that I am much better off celebrating than lamenting. What is the cost of this rich anal sexuality? A diminished virility—at times, the very thought of mounting and thrusting exhausts me.

I do not claim to have thoroughly vanquished the interpretive impulse. While the anus and the phallus are, upon good materialist analysis, equally mere meat, I am still embedded in a culture in which they are laden with heavy symbolic meaning. I do suspect, however, that the reason I do not despair or succumb to sexual anxiety is that I have been able to navigate the symbolic minefield of modern sexuality on the crutches of the theories presented in this book. Buddhist anti-essentialism turned so many monsters into cartoons, feminist critique destabilized the phallic hierarchy, and the playful vault of phenomenological space invited me to revel in play. While I have fallen short of the classical erotic goal of "finding my other half," I take solace in having been able to validate and comfort a few others who struggled with their own nonnormativity, and I have been able to enjoy heights of rapture with the right people in our mutual attraction—when we have stumbled into each other's orbits.

Nonetheless, this sexuality puts me in an awkward position. Like most people, I do have a certain preferences. My "complex of attraction" involves a female partner, and I would prefer her to be trans. In chapter 1 I tried to express some nonsexual reasons for this, and here I will tread into the difficult terrain of articulating sexual reasons. I note unabashedly that I have enjoyed sexual encounters with all genders and sexed bodies, including cis-men. I do not, however, consider myself gay, and even the term bi does not quite resonate with me. To dip into the postmodern alphabet soup of identity, perhaps something like "hetero-romantic contextually-pansexual" fits the bill. I have always valued discretion and privacy, but if asked specifically about something, I would not shy from sharing details. I am relatively unburdened by shame and confusion, at least on these matters. Yet it's a sexuality that is particularly messy for others to understand, and one that is a target for all kinds of assumptions and projections.

For many, it is unfathomable to decouple male anality from the metaphysical category of the Gay Man, a caricature who plays an important role in our cultural history. Moreover, the disparagement of gay bottoms, which is linked to misogyny, has been discussed widely in LGBT literature. A bottom's sexuality is too close to the stereotypical woman's—a sexuality of "passivity" and "weakness."[2] The gay bottom, the trope suggests, denies his gift of masculinity and sovereignty.[3] Only very recently, with the development of the sex-positive movement, have cis-partnered, heterosexual men been given some license to explore anal stimulation with their wives without the accusation of sublimated homosexuality. As a cis male transam bottom in a relationship with a top trans woman, the hetero-gay binary simply does not pertain to my own experience; it is an absurdity for others to be mire themselves thinking about. ,.

I can only speak for myself, but we might all speak our voices. This motivates sexologist Zhana Vrangalova's *Casual Sex Project*,[4] an open online forum encouraging people from all walks of life to recount their sexual escapades, simply to shine a light on the diversity of sexual experience.

The nuances of sexuality should be voiced because I sometimes feel more judged than questioned about mine. When asked to justify my transam orientation, how is it possible to escape being labeled a fetishist? My first riposte may be to suggest that as a cis man, does the heteronormative cis woman or the bottom trans woman not reduce me to my phallus? Is it not the condition upon which all further interaction depends? Is it not exactly what is inferred by my masculine presentation? There is no formula for what follows. Throughout this book I have made a case that sexualities based on metaphysical essences, synecdoche, or interpretation are open doors to pain, so I must craft my own personal, aesthetic, phenomenological message.

What of my preference for a woman who has a penis? The most satisfying answer for myself is a phenomenological one. When I close my eyes and slip back into the sweet memories of those best sexual moments where the discursive, interpreting monkey-mind melts away into relaxation and union, I often recall the rapture of a feminine, phallus-bearing lover. Further weakening the symbolic power of the phallus, I know that my sexuality is not strongly visual. I enjoy the tactile sensations: textures, wetness, swelling. I have less of a predilection for standard BDSM. The assumption that bottoming involves degradation or humiliation is a projection from common notions of masculinity and femininity, and what acts are indexed to them. What I'm after is the feeling of relaxation that comes from letting my lover in, and letting go, in the occasionally intense *calm*, the silent, nondiscursive moment. The process of getting there may be quite painful, yet the only cure for that pain may be deeper levels of relaxation. At these heights, the pain is rendered vivid and directionless, belonging to nobody.

Of course preferences are preferences, and we should be vigilant against attempts to house our preferences in sacrosanct walls. The dogmas that arise from this uncritical thinking are sandbags in the great dike against sexual freedom. At the heart of the problem is the metaphysical link posited between Male and Female, Masculine and Feminine, and certain sexual acts, as if the acts are truly manifestations, emanations of, the eternal ideals of Man and Woman.

We still approach sex as idealists. We revert to a primitive and childish kind of discourse—boys do certain things and girls do other things, and that's just the way it is. We embrace old pairings like passivity = feminine and aggressiveness = masculine; you can only be one or the other. These couplings have the weight of history behind them, but we know that history's habits are often misguided. Our sexualities plod down these furrows with a vague reassurance from the patriarchy that they will be rewarded.

For a long time, I have noticed that I do not achieve or maintain an erection with the facility the heteronormative paradigm expects of me. Certainly stress and self-consciousness have sabotaged past attempts to play the role of the virile heteronormative top. Lovers' disappointment many times having turned to shaming me has played a role in turning me off further. But I believe there is more than psychological tripwires at play, and there is something tragic about the entire framework of "erectile dysfunction." It is well documented how the function of the penis depends on a vast complex of factors that are hormonal, cardiovascular, and psychological.[5] An erection is an expression of a psychophysical constitution, not of one's desire. The only thing that makes "erectile dysfunction" "unfortunate" is that it disappoints the expectations of "those who view erections as the sole measure of a partner's desire for them" (Bussell). Sometimes conditions yield an erection, and then intercourse feels good, but it is not some mechanism by which to achieve a metaphysically sexual climax. I do not always want genital orgasm when I bottom. Then, the anus is the epicenter, but the feelings emanate from there through the torso and to the ends of my limbs. My entire body buzzes, tenses up, quivers, and relaxes. It is total. In comparison, at least for me, the orgasm is so small, the energies involved so limited, the sensation seldom ripples much past the limited territory of the groin. And I can masturbate myself to genital orgasm, yet the full-body energies engaged in anal sexuality require a partner who helps stimulate them.

Simone de Beauvoir has aptly described the way so-called male and female sexual behaviors carry millennia of dogma within them.

> For man, the passage from childhood sexuality to maturity is relatively simple: erotic pleasure is objectified; now instead of being realized in his immanent presence, this erotic pleasure is intended for a transcendent being. The erection is the expression of this need; with penis, hands, mouth, with his whole body, the man reaches out to his partner, but he remains at the heart of this activity . . . he projects himself toward the other without losing his autonomy; feminine flesh is prey for him, and he seizes in the woman the attributes his sensuality requires of any object . . . The act of love finds its unity in its natural culmination; orgasm. Coitus has a specific physiological aim; in

ejaculation the male releases burdensome secretions; after orgasm, the male feels complete relief regularly accompanied by pleasure. And, of course, pleasure is not the only aim; it is often followed by disappointment: the need has disappeared rather than having been satisfied (de Beauvoir 383).

This statement captures my own experience of the fleeting, falsely affirming, oft dispiriting character of typical coital sex. But we forget that acts are just acts. Nothing inheres in them designating them as "for man" or "for woman." The acts described above are not "for man" because they carry some metaphysical essence, but are only so because of the historical habit of affixing meaning, of *interpreting* acts. In the description above, I recognize a kind of sex I've had because it has felt expected of me as a man attracted to women. But it is not *my* sexuality as an individual; it is not how I, given freedom, choose to offer my energies or achieve satisfaction.

When I do top, or even occasionally enjoy a dominant role, I do *not* feel more of a "man" for it at all. I enjoy it for the excitement achieved by the shared encounter. It takes a rare person to inspire a dominant energy in me of any naturalness. When I have done it to be a good sport, I have found that I have to expend a lot of energy thinking of just the right thing to do, the right balance, the buildup. It's a choreography that I find exhausting. My more dominant top partners have explained to me that it's the opposite for them—the choreography comes to them spontaneously and they relax into the adventure they are crafting. None of this has anything to do with metaphysical Man or Woman; top/bottom, Dom/sub are performative roles; they may seem more or less "natural" to us, but that naturalness is purely aleatory, the runoff of our peculiar constitution.

When de Beauvoir describes "woman's sexuality," I recognize much more of my own than in the previous description of male sexuality. However, she doesn't follow her reasoning to its conclusion; she doesn't recognize that she is just describing a *kind* of sexuality that could belong to *any*one. It is not so much that "woman's eroticism is far more complex and reflects the complexity of her situation"; most of us have complex sexualities, many of us are in complex situations. In contrast to the desultory coitus of the stereotypical male she described earlier, her account of "feminine" sexuality is richly erotic.

> . . . There is a surge in her that ceaselessly falls and rises: it is this surge that creates the spell that perpetuates desire. But the balance between ardor and abandon is easy to destroy. Male desire is tension; it can invade a body where nerves and muscles are taut . . . [For women] the violence of uncontrolled tendencies the absence of inhibition—physical as well as moral—permits a concentration of all living energy into the sexual act (de Beauvoir 390).

As a man, I say damn the "tension" that is supposed to characterize my desire. Let there be a "surge in [*me*] that ceaselessly falls and rises: it is this surge that creates the spell that perpetuates desire." Let inhibitions fall away. Let me have the "intensity" in the following passage that is supposedly cut off from my sex.

> Feminine arousal can reach an intensity unknown by man. Male desire is violent but localized, and he comes out of it—except perhaps in the instant of ejaculation—conscious of himself; woman, by contrast, undergoes a real alienation; for many, this metamorphosis is the most voluptuous and definitive moment of love; but it also has a magical and frightening side. The woman he is holding in his arms appears so absent from herself, so much in the throes

of turmoil, that the man may feel afraid of her. The upheaval she feels is a far more radical transmutation than the male's aggressive frenzy. (de Beauvoir 405).

Some of my lovers, particularly cis females who topped me, have said that they felt like the male in de Beauvoir's depiction. So absorbed was I in the feeling she was giving me, it seemed I was in another place. This perspective was new and exciting for them as they realized how they must look when they are in the same "throes of turmoil."

Here is an example of how we cannot dwell in the space of phenomenological innocence indefinitely. After these throes of turmoil, these nondiscursive heights, meanings and interpretations will inevitably trickle back in; but now they will have shifted a bit and I will have to grapple with the subtle ways in which I am relating to people and acts as symbols. A parallel can be made here that will surely offend some of the puritanical sensibilities of some Buddhists I know. In the Indo-Tibetan Buddhist tradition, there is an extensive discourse about the difference between *meditation* and *post-meditation*. In the Tibetan language, the terms are *sgoms*, which has the sense of cultivation or guided habituation, and *rjes thob*, which, literally rendered as "subsequent attainment," means the sense of the *aftermath* or *wake* of an applied session of meditation. The meditation session itself sometimes leads to a state of absorption (*rting nges 'dzin*) that disrupts or de-habituates us from our ordinary, discursive, interpretive furrow. A Tibetan idiom calls this "tearing down the hut of ordinary mind." These disruptions irrupt into a richer subsequent reality. Yet they are not fireworks. The rich tradition of *śmatha* (calm-abiding) and *vipaśyana* (insight) meditation do not aim for visions and revelations, but rather the shedding of the wool over our eyes, that thick matte that covers the nakedness of appearances, that causes us to look beyond a thing for its meaning, that causes us to look at our fellows, our lovers, as conduits of some transcendental essence.

Role-reversal, the reversal of perspective, and the inversion of traditional, habitual performances—these undeniably form some of what appeals to me about bottoming for a woman. My aesthetic preference for a woman is very significant, but nearly as important is the vague, almost unconscious awareness that in this coupling we have cast away a stifling, moribund paradigm, and we have achieved the heights of pleasure, literally and figuratively, through the back door. A top trans woman challenges all our assumptions about masculinity and femininity alike.

Whether vaginal intercourse is, as de Beauvoir described, "violent but localized," we can all turn keys unto our own and others' dignified nakedness; we can take leave of ourselves in the throes of turmoil; giving and receiving with our partner, we can all experience radical transmutation and aggressive frenzy. They are both our birthright, and somewhere in us both poles exist. The means of glorious satisfaction are spontaneously present; we can find them and know them; the territories of our desires are not to be read from maps but traveled in the flesh; the people who appear to us are not to be interpreted but seen with bright eyed wonder, reverence, and awe.

ENDNOTES

PREFACE

1. This term, which has now been adopted by the Oxford English Dictionary, designates "a person whose sense of personal identity corresponds to the sex and gender assigned to him or her at birth", i.e., a "non-trans" person, which has the unwanted entailment that being non-trans is the default, normative human condition. The Latin prefix *cis* means "on this side of" and it is the etymological opposite of trans. While the term is not new, its popularization is a major linguistic achievement since for a long time we did not have a clear way to refer to non-trans people in general. "Normal" certainly wasn't appropriate, and "real" was even worse. For a while "biological" and "genetic" were in vogue, until it was demonstrated that, indeed, trans people are just as biological and genetic as any other living organism. (For more on etymology and adoption see Green 2015.)
2. I will interrogate this problematic binary category throughout the book. At present, I intend "hetero" as the way I have generally been perceived, as well how I perceived myself until I became more critical of the category. For an excellent discussion of this issue, see Tompkins 2011, p. 90 (under the heading "*Read as Straight: Language and (In)visibility*").
3. Denoting or relating to a person whose sense of personal identity and gender does not correspond with the sex they were assigned at birth.
4. Whose work fueled the TERF movement (trans-exclusionary radical feminists). See Kappel 2015; Jones.
5. Bettcher 2015
6. This was the headline of *Time Magazine*, May 29, 2014, which featured a cover photo of trans actor and activist Laverne Cox.
7. Thomas Matt has written two short but thoughtful articles (Matt 2013, 2015). Also see Rohrbach. Perry Gruber, a cis-het-male transam runs a blog and podcast podcast *The Transamorous Network*. Other than Gruber's postings and for-sale pamphlets, however, there are no other cis-het transams speaking out on that platform—the nineteen-episode podcast features only one transamorous cis male guest, and he does not give his full name. Dan Savage holds a short conversation with a transamorous man (Savage). There are also thoughtful but, ironically, mostly anonymous sites called *Transoriented.com* and *TransOrientedMen.com* containing a few short articles and support resources. Just before submitting this book for publication, I discovered what seems to be the first transam monograph entitled *Trans-Oriented: A Guide to Love and Relationships for Men who Love Transsexual Women* by Michael David Freel. While frank and honest, the author expresses that the book is "targeted toward men and thus needs to be a little blunter than a book that would be targeted toward women." He dispenses general dating advice and traces the arch from "The Horny Troll" to the "TGentleman," offering the gloss "A gentleman is an alpha male." He also offers practical advice to men for coming out as "trans-oriented," much of which is timely and sound. However, it is unabashedly written from a non-feminist, non-queer, completely personal perspective that arrives at insights

like "In the trans world, bottoms are generally not seen as real men. They're weak and not interested in real relationship [sic]." Those with a feminist leaning will likely find it quite aggravating and hard to relate to. *Trans-Oriented* does, however, end with the postscript, "Remember this: TGirls and TGentlemen are all individuals. As much as I've tried to give you guidance and explain the reality of being Trans-Oriented, your story is going to be different." Meanwhile, there is no shortage of cis women writing about their relationships with trans women, though they usually focus on the dramatic shift that occurs when their cis male partner transitions into a trans woman (Boyd 2007; Fabian 2014; Sands 2016 among so many others). Trans men and trans women have written compellingly of their romantic and sexual relationships with trans women (Diamond 2011; Serano 2007, 2013, Cromwell 1999, and the prolific corpus of Patrick Califia (e.g., 2003). Giselle Renarde (2013) has written well-received cis/trans lesbian erotica—my search for feministic rather than fetishistic cis-het-male/trans-female erotica has been fruitless. Tam Sanger has written a commendable academic tome on trans partnerships of all kinds (Sanger 2010). For cis-het transamorous men, the only venues for public discourse remain the perennially problematic *Reddit* and hypersexualized forums like the horribly named *Hung Angels*. The editors of a recent collections of trans love stories concedes, "At this historical juncture, much of the public writing about partnering with trans people is by the cisgender female partners of trans masculine men and nonbinary people—a phenomena no doubt influenced by cultural messages about both femininity and masculinity" (Johnson & Garrison 2015).

8. For a wonderful survey see Bettcher, "Feminist Perspectives on Trans Issues" (2009/2014 revised).
9. For critiques of cis "experts trying to steer the discourse see Serano 2007; Hale 1997; Boyd; Stone; Stryker; Spade; Towle & Morgan.
10. The psychological theories and medical practices prescribed by Dr. Harry Benjamin, for example, has affected the lives of virtually every contemporary trans woman (see Stryker & Whittle 2006).
11. See Kappel 2016
12. See Baldwin; Delgado; Roediger.
13. Throughout the book I use the term *transam* as an abbreviation for this type of person.
14. "The T" is an expression in the trans world that refers to the revelation of one's trans status. "Does he know the T?" "Did you tell him the T?" etc. It often marks the end of a burgeoning flirtation. For a discussion of this see Mock 2011.
15. Many writers in transgender studies have justifiably criticized a habitual conflation of trans identity issues with issues of sexuality (see Salamon 46). The goal of *Trans*Am*, however, is not to develop a general trans theory, but to explore and to interrogate the phenomenon of cis men who find love with trans women.
16. German *Mitsein* ("being with") is an important term in existentialist philosophy, and one particularly germane to a project of critical cisness (see Wheeler for a discussion of the term). The term characterizes human existence as never autonomous but always implicated with others. Since the very structure of our existence entails our interdependence with others, we impoverish our existence when we deny or fail to appreciate this interdependence.

17. For example, North Carolina just passed HB2, widely known as the "Bathroom Bill," which relies on a view of trans people as sexual predators who lurk in public restrooms waiting for opportunities to assault young cis people (see Graham).
18. Many of our greatest trans writers, such as Bornstein, Feinberg, and Stone, were reacting against trans-exclusionary-radical-feminists' (TERFS) attempts to exclude them from second wave feminism in the 1970s and 80s. As lesbian feminists themselves, they attacked such dogmatism and revolutionized what it meant to be a feminist, or a woman, paving the way for transfeminism and third-wave feminism (for a survey of this see Jacques 2015: ch.4). These latter movements combined, in the 1990s, with the burgeoning field of queer theory. They further deconstructed the old binary categories of man and woman, focusing instead on the diversity of individuals, the intersection of class, race, gender, violence, and a myriad of other factors that condition a person's identity. Many of the most influential writers of this generation (Bettcher, Califia, Finney-Boylan, Koyama, Serano) identify either as lesbian, bi, or queer. Trans men of various sexualities are also well represented (Andrews, Bono, Hale, Kailey, Prosser, etc.). More recently, hetero trans women such as Hill and Mock have published excellent memoirs; however, as memoirs, they cannot possibly represent the entire diverse population of trans women.
19. I have tried my best not to too badly disappoint the expectations set by C. Jacob Hale in his invaluable, generous piece "Suggested Rules for Non-Transsexuals Writing about Transsexuals, Transsexuality, Transsexualism, or Trans ____."
20. In an ancient Indian parable, a group of blind men are asked to describe an elephant. One man is positioned near the trunk and he says, "It is like a snake." Another at the foot declares, "It is like a stump," etc. It illustrates the limitations of individual perspectives and the need to allow the thing itself to express its own truth.

INTRODUCTION

1. See Harmony 2016 for a particularly harsh condemnation of this kind of man.
2. While revising this manuscript, I discovered Michael David Freel's recent book *Trans-Oriented*, in which he wrote virtually the same thing. I must give him credit for preceding me here. Rather than replacing my wording with his, I reproduce his here as evidence that this may be a common observation among transamorous men—perhaps we will hear this trope again and again in transamorous discourse. His passage reads, "Most TGirls, just like everybody else, want to have someone special in their life to love and to love them back. Unfortunately, many of them are chasing a fairy tale that goes something like this: She meets a tall, handsome stranger who finds her attractive. He asks her out and she accepts. They begin dating and things go very well, and they begin to fall in love. She realizes she must tell him the truth and eventually works up the nerve. He's shocked and uneasy at first but realizes that he loves her anyway and is willing to overlook or put up with her T. They fall madly in love, and the T doesn't matter. They pretend it's not even there and live happily ever after. While this fantasy does come true sometimes, it is, by far, the exception rather than the rule. And even if it does come true, I say it's not good enough. Being trans is not something that should just be accepted or put up with or

ignored. It should not be 'I love you despite who you are.' It should be 'I love you because of who you are.'"
3. For the uninitiated, "top" and "bottom" refer to the more active partner applying techniques and the more passive partner who receives them.
4. Mock 2011, 2014, 2015 attest to it.
5. This is a useful neologism popular in the kink community. It refers the negative reaction we have toward certain sexual acts—a reaction that is almost always irrational, visceral, and which marks a boundary. Kink culture encourages us to be aware of what "squicks" us and to recognize squicking as real but personal, private, irrational—nothing we wish to universalize or compel others to share.
6. For a nearly identical childhood story by a transamorous cis lesbian woman see Anderson-Minshall (2013a).
7. Sapiosexual: Of a person finding intelligence sexually attractive or arousing (Oxford).
8. A person who does not experience sexual attraction or sexual pleasure unless they have formed a strong emotional connection with their partner.
9. Much more on this later.
10. In the kink community, "vanilla" means conventional, not kinky.
11. A "tranny chaser" is a man with an objectifying or fetishistic lust for trans women. For an illuminating discussion of this see Milloy, Reid.
12. He is a comically menacing character (think: Donald Trump) from the TV show *The Simpsons*.
13. I say, "when appropriate," because the issue of when and how to communicate sexual preferences in the transamorous context is a thorny one I will discuss at the end of this chapter.
14. For a timeless piece on the relationship between stress and sexual performance, and the need for patience, compassion, and a sense of humor in sexual dynamics, see Montaigne's "On the Power of the Imagination" (Montaigne, 1958).
15. For a survey of the history of trans women in the media see Serano 2007: ch. 2. Also see Magdalena; Silverman.
16. On the adventures of online dating as trans women see Daniari; Edison (who interestingly points out that cis women do this to her too); Harmony; Lees 2015; Milloy; Reid; Willis
17. Alternatives are the poorly organized BDSM-focused Fetlife.com and CollarMe.com, or the random salacious Craigslist "casual encounters" section—not really great places to just meet someone for drinks.
18. The meaning of the term "vers" is versatile, meaning someone who both tops and bottoms; the meaning of "vers btm" is versatile bottom, who prefers to bottom but will top.
19. On bottom shaming see Johnson; Lowder; Michael 2015, 2016; Moore; and Rodriguez-Jimenez. For an example of transamorous bottom shaming, see Freel: "In the trans world, bottoms are generally not seen as real men. They're weak and not interested in real relationship [sic]" (2016: "Tops and Bottoms").

CHAPTER ONE
1. See Harmony.
2. For a discussion of the lambasting of a cis female partner of a trans man for expressing such an affinity, see Anderson-Minshall 2013b.

3. I will not dignify the T-word with a mention.
4. For many reasons, including the author's ontological limits as a cis man and the specifically problematic situation of a cis man's attraction to trans women, this book narrowly circumscribes its purview; consequently, for the sake of convenience, the book uses "cis-trans" as shorthand to reference "cis *man*-trans *woman*" unless stated otherwise.
5. Avery Tompkins 2014.
6. Avery Tompkins interviews a variety of cis female partners of trans males and she describes two of their attitudes in the following way. "Shawna says that it is not okay for someone to seek out relationships with trans people, certainly not more than one trans person, and we can infer that the 'ulterior motive' she mentions here refers to sexual activity, which is off-limits. She goes on to say: 'If someone wanted to call me it . . . they would be ignorant because my boyfriend is the first trans person I've been with.' In other words, she cannot be a tranny chaser because she has dated only one trans person. Beth suggested that it is possibly okay for someone to have a preference for dating trans people, but Shawna claims otherwise. If you like a person and find out later they are trans, that is okay—'you happen to be trans'—but you cannot like someone for being trans" (2014: 771).
7. "Intimate Allies: Identity, Community, and Everyday Activism Among Cisgender People with Trans-Identified Partners" (Tompkins 2011).
8. "'There's No Chasing Involved': Cis/Trans Relationships, 'Tranny Chasers,' and the Future of a Sex-Positive Trans Politics" (Tompkins 2014).
9. I use "their" whenever I am uncertain of a referent's preferred pronoun.
10. Christin Scarlett Milloy, "Beware the Chasers: 'Admirers' Who Harass Trans People." *Outward* (Oct. 2, 2014).
11. Charley Reid, "My Trans Identity Is Not A Fetish." *The Establishment*. Sep. 15, 2016.
12. Anecdotally, I have witnessed some of my trans women friends go through such an experience, and it seems to be the kind of experience Milloy and Reid are reacting to.
13. Indeed, many of the most common patterns have vernacular labels: "yellow fever," "jungle fever," "size queen," "rice queen," "potato queen," "chubby chaser," and of course "tranny chaser."
14. Beauvoir; Bettcher 2012.
15. Laqueuer; Richardson.
16. See Roiphe.
17. See Chandra.
18. See Daoud.
19. I feel compelled to clarify that these were never *my* students!
20. See Ailith; Biko; Roberts 2016a&b; Ross; Taffet.
21. It has been noted that the alleged abuser was also criticized by other cis men on the panel, including Thomas Matt who has been favorably cited in this book as a cis ally to trans women, and who, not immaterially, happens to be the partner of the courageous trans activist Jennicet Guttierrez, not known to suffer hypocrisy and exploitation lightly. (Biko).
22. T4T: "trans for trans." This is an idiom derived from Craigslist hookup culture, where people provide acronyms as keys for what they are looking for sexually: m4w (man for woman), t4m (trans for man) etc.

23. Anderson-Minshall, Belawski, Boyd, Freel, and Matt 2013 all express similar sentiments.
24. Heidegger coined the German term *Geworfenheit* ("thrownness") to express the arbitrariness of our place in the world. We have not been *put here* by a benevolent and omniscient creator who has a plan for us; rather, we have been *thrown*, by chance, into a situation that does not make much sense.
25. Nietzsche admonished philosophy for its pretenses to ethical science, exhorting us to turn our lives into art instead. In *The Gay Science*, he writes, "*One thing is needful*. 'Giving style' to one's character—a great and rare art! It is exercised by those who see all the strengths and weaknesses of their own natures and then comprehend them in an artistic plan until everything appears as art and reason, and even weakness delights the eye. Here a large mass of second nature has been added; there a piece of original nature has been removed: both by long practice and daily labor. Here the ugly that could not be removed is hidden; there it has been reinterpreted and made sublime . . . For one thing is needful: that a human being *attain* his satisfaction with himself . . . only then is a human being at all tolerable to behold. Whoever is dissatisfied with himself is always ready to revenge himself therefore; we others will be his victims" (§ 290). Nietzsche directly opposes aesthetic to ethical values, but I propose we can admit the distinction without entailing the precedence of one over another.
26. Sartre imagines Genet thinking, "I am a victim of a lack of understanding, of a spontaneous aversion which in the end exiles me definitively. Certain people find my presence on earth suspect, and their hostile attitude thrusts me back into my secret" (206). "Genet's originality lies in his wanting to be, and in his being the non-synthetic unity of his contradictions" (Sartre: 248).
27. Sartre speculates that, "If Genet is a 'nature,' everything is comprised in that nature, including the movement he makes to turn to it and lay claim to it. If Genet has the power to claim his essence, then he also has the power to reject it, to change it. He is free, and his nature is only a myth or a decoy"(61).
28. In addition to the many memoirs cited throughout, see Schultz (chapter 2) and Erickson-Schroth for a compilation of transition narratives.
29. I will discuss, in depth, the separate sexual question in chapter 7.
30. Serano, a biologist by trade, writes, "As a feminist, I look forward to a time when we finally move beyond the idea that biology is destiny, and recognize that the most important differences that exist between women and men in our society are the different meanings that we place onto one another's bodies"(2007: 94).
31. This is discussed in many places, for example: Alder; Lovaas; Marech; Nardizzi 172; Serano 2013, chapter 1; Stryker 2006, xii.
32. This is not a claim I have seen anyone make explicitly and publicly, although some examples I have noted come close. On the other side, Serano (2009a&b; 2013b), Mock (2013), Anderson-Minshall (2013a&b) all write against stigmatizing transamorous partners. Personally, I have listened to some of my trans female friends argue that having an affinity for trans women is indeed inherently fetishizing and objectifying. Not long ago, two of my trans female friends and I were sharing our respective dating woes and one of them said, rather hopelessly, "I can't stand guys who are into trans girls," to which my other friend added exasperatedly, "Yes, basically I'm not interested in anyone who would

be interested in me." They knew I would not take these remarks personally, and that I would find them somewhat hyperbolic, so I had to ask, "Then what are you supposed to do?" Needless to say, we came up with no answers that evening; the consensus was to keep slogging through horrible dates until maybe one day, miraculously, someone isn't awful. This book contributes to our ongoing conversation.

33. I first heard this term circa 2008 from my friend Eric Miclette. "Transamory" can be found in the *Urban Dictionary* and "Transamorous" has become fairly widely used (for example, Anderson-Minshall; Belawski & Sojka; Fischer & Seidman; Erickson-Schroth; Boyd) but "Transam" is less frequent (Anderson-Minshall a&b; Dawes; Boyd 2013; Gruber).
34. For another etymological analysis see Dawes.
35. On "postmodernism" Gary Aylesworth writes, "That postmodernism is indefinable is a truism. However, it can still be described as a set of critical, strategic, and rhetorical practices employing concepts such as difference, repetition, the trace, the simulacrum, and hyperreality to destabilize other concepts such as presence, identity, historical progress, epistemic certainty, and the univocity of meaning"(Aylesworth). For a discussion that speaks to the modern and postmodern proliferation of taxonomies and terms, see Taylor (1998: 1).
36. This is behind the Christian Right and the Republican Party's "Defense of Marriage" insisting that "marriage is between one man and one woman" full stop (Prupis). It is also the view expressed by Kevin Williamson of *The National Review* (2013,2014).
37. Monosexual: being or related to someone who has sexual attraction to or relations with one sex or gender only.
38. See Eisner; Serano 2012 & 2013; Klein; Scott-Clary;
39. See Eisner p. 49.There is also the acronym QUILTBAG: Queer/Questioning, Undecided, Intersex, Lesbian, Trans, Bisexual, Asexual, and Gay (see Adler; Lee; Rios).
40. Serano 2013.
41. For a discussion of this see Schmalbach.
42. Serrano 2013: 88.
43. Serano 2007: chapter 15; Serano 2013: chapter 7.
44. Bornstein and Serano are examples. Also see Brighe; Shelley (2014, 2016).
45. On straight transamorous men, see Gubb 2013, 2014; Mauk; Mock 2013. For academic studies addressing the variety of queer and straight transamorous partnerships, see Lenning 2008 and Tompkins 2007, 2014. My remarks here about the social habits of hetero identified transamorous men are largely based on my own experience, as well as anecdotally based on hundreds of conversations of men I've met who identify similarly.
46. There is a slogan that reads "Not gay as in happy but queer as in fuck you!" "Queer" has a long history—from derogatory slur to reclaimed badge of honor—but since its reclamation through queer theory and activism, it has generally denoted the rejection of "straight" or normative, sometimes including homo-normative, and dissatisfaction with extant taxonomies, categories, labels etc. See Rand p. 156; Giaimo; Zanin; Bailey & Leylabi; Katz; Ziyad.
47. For a thorough and excellent discussion of activist potential of trans partners, see Tomkins 2011. For example, they write, "While many partners refuse

to call themselves 'activists,' my research illustrates that they are engaging in actions that contribute to social change around trans issues. Everyday activism is often about individuals working to carve out a more habitable everyday life, and this type of micro-activism, or everyday resistance, is often routinely part of the lives of cisgender people with trans partners. While education is often not considered to be activism, I illustrate how it contributes to social change in ways that other forms of everyday activism and resistance do and argue that 'educational advocacy' is one type of trans ally activism in which cis partners engage" (2011: 37).

48. For academic studies on this phenomenon, see Lenning and Tompkins. For journalistic examples see Mock 2013; Fairchild; Serano 2013b.
49. See Gubb 2013.
50. Serano 2013: chapter 8.
51. See Clark-Flory; Hsu; Mauk.
52. See Michel Onfray (2015) for his notion of "lighthearted eros."
53. Dawes 2013. It must be noted that the author did not coin the term, since I heard it used loosely around NYC circa 2008.
54. http://transamorousnetwork.com/transamorous-men/i-like-trans-am/.
I confess that I had similar thoughts when I first heard the term many years ago. I found that the term transam, with its association with Burt Reynolds ridiculous romp of a film *Smokey and the Bandit* provided a comfortingly masculine context within which I could edify some of my more jocular, staunchly cis-het, borderline-nohomo-uttering friends and acquaintances about the nuances of non-heternormative sexualities. The Pontiac motif is also employed at the header of Jacob Anderson-Minshall's article "My Wife Is a Trans Am."
55. See Hamblin; Holloway; Marcotte.
56. In 1970 the radical feminist Shulamith Firestone caused a stir by advocating universal androgyny in her book *The Dialectic of Sex*. Subsequently, many prominent feminists criticized the viability of this vision (Tong).
57. Serano 2013: 157.
58. Kimberly Reed's excellent film *Prodigal Sons* knows this kind of masculinity has no permanence either. The filmmaker, growing up in Montana, was the quintessential prom-king and star quarterback and eventually transitions to live as a woman.
59. Serano 2007: chapter 19.
60. Serano 2013: chapter 9.
61. Mock 2013; Fairchild.
62. See Di Dourjée's article "'I Love Trannies': Boxer Yusaf Mack Fights for His Attraction to Trans Women."
63. See Serano 2007: chapter 5.
64. Schmalbach; Tompkins.
65. For the most comprehensive survey of the population (still only 205 men), see Hsu. In this survey, "51 percent identified as straight, 41 percent called themselves bisexual and a piddling six men ID'd as gay" (Clark-Flory).

CHAPTER TWO

1. Seen in the early calls for justice and equal rights by Wollstonecraft (xiii-xiv),

Olympe de Gouges, Mill, and Mill (who came out of the Epicurean/Utilitarian tradition in which the amelioration of pain should guide *everything*). Second wave feminism does not deviate from this central concern of improving the livability of women's lives in a crushingly patriarchal world (Beauvoir, Friedan) nor do third-wave feminists as different as Mary Daly and bell hooks, who offers the apothegm, "Feminism is a movement to end sexism, sexist exploitation, and oppression" (bell hooks 2000: viii).

2. For example, in Susan Stryker's foreword to the valuable *The Transgender Studies Reader*, she writes, "Regardless of the fact that trans identities are now more available, the problems of being trans have by no means been resolved. In many parts of the world, having a trans identity still puts a person at risk of discrimination, violence, and even death" (xi). This central concern about decreasing the frustration of being (trans) and of finding ways to make being (trans) joyful is articulated more personally in Thalia Mae Bettcher's "Other Worldly Philosophy."

3. Paltrul Rinpoche describes this aspect of existence in the following way. "We experience suffering upon suffering when, before one suffering is over, we are subjected to another. We get leprosy, and then we break out in boils too; and then as well as breaking out in boils we get injured. Our father dies and then our mother dies soon afterward. We are pursued by enemies and, on top of that, a loved one dies; and so forth" (78–79).

4. See Anderson-Minshall 2013a; Mock 2013; and Tompkins 2014.

5. Chaz Bono discusses, in his memoir, his mother Cher's sense of loss after his transition. ". . . I could understand that my mom was grieving the loss of the person she perceived her daughter to be. However, I was still very much alive, and missing her" (ch. 14). He also describes a melancholic sense of lost time. "Along with going through all of the changes that have happened as a result of transitioning, I have also experienced a deep sense of loss and profound sadness for the forty years of life I spent inside of the wrong body" (afterword). Andrews (ch. 10) and Hill (ch. 10) discuss similar feelings in their memoirs. It is also addressed in Girshik (ch. 6).

6. Gampopa 95-96.

7. Patrul 79.

8. Arin Andrews writes, "I lived in some weird dimension, peering out at the rest of existence from the strange prison of a body that didn't match my mind"(ch.3). Mock writes, "*Being who I really am will lead to rejection*. Concealing who you are warps your sense of self and heightens feelings of hopelessness about ever being able to be your true self. A defeatist feeling loomed over me, telling me that no one would ever understand and accept me. I began believing that people, including my family and friends, would be disgusted by me, and these new belief systems anchored in the shame that I internalized from the world around me led to further isolation"(2014:ch. 7). Finney-Boylan reflects, "How is it, I wondered, that some people manage to integrate their lives and live in the moment, while other become stuck, become Exes, haunting their own lives like ghosts?"(2008: part 1 "Dirty Deeds"). Katie Rain Hill recalls her early dysphoria in similar terms: "For me it was more than discomfort. It was a profound alienation from my body that I had no idea how to articulate" (2014: ch. 5). It need not always be deeply melancholic; a passage from Serano's

Whipping Girl captures the subtle introspective phenomenology of the "lash in the eye" quite well. "I felt more like I was floating in a little dinghy that had been recently released from the dock I had been anchored to my whole life; and now I was being tossed about on an ocean of other people's perceptions of me. And while I was definitely searching for a place where I could feel at home in my own body, I was no longer quite sure what that place might look like or what I might call it when I finally arrived" (part II, ch. 10).
9. Countless books on Buddhist theory discuss it: see Anderson; Bodhi; Emmanuel; Harvey; and Keown.
10. A common metaphor in Buddhist meditation discourses that connotes the possibility of formerly troubling mental processes to simply undo themselves when we no longer engage with them and fuel them (for uses, see Tsoknyi 151; Van Schaik 109).
11. An idiom in Tibetan Buddhism for breaking up the habitual psychological patterns and conceptual attachments that have caused us so much trouble; see Chagdud.
12. Referred to traditionally as the "Three Trainings" or "Three Wisdom Tools" (see Chogye; Dalai Lama 97; Molk 235; Ray 30).
13. In her influential volume of feminist Buddhist scholarship, *Buddhism After Patriarchy*, Rita Gross uses these terms—"accurate" and "usable"—to guide her examination of the Buddhist tradition's conflicted history (where we find "usable," feministic theory juxtaposed with an "inaccurate" historiography that largely effaces women's voices).
14. Hanson; Pittman; Schwartz; Stafford; Steinmetz 2015.
15. For a discussion of this see Boellstorff, et al.: "Decolonizing Transgender."
16. Jean-Paul Sartre's analysis of the Other's gaze and the self's shame in his 1943 *Being and Nothingness* eloquently makes this point. Moreover, the course of history presents innumerable cases of tribes, ethnicities, and whole civilizations coming to naught in catastrophic ends.
17. Slavoj Žižek/Sophie Fiennes' film *The Pervert's Guide to Ideology* is an entertaining and edifying examination of the occurrence.
18. Plato's view of women is more ambivalent than Aristotle's, who leans much more on the side of biological essentialism. For a detailed discussion of their views on women see Smith 1983.
19. This episteme, of course, is only satisfactory for cisgender people and others squarely ensconced in various normativities.
20. These include the TERF movement (trans-exclusionary-radical feminism) cited earlier and discussed in Erikson-Schroth (568).
21. ". . . The transsexual does not really change sex at all. But this does not mean that gender is immutable; it means that men cannot become women via hormones and surgery. My view is that . . . the male-to-female transsexual is a "fantastic woman," the incarnation of a male fantasy of feeling like a woman trapped in a man's body, the fantasy rendered flesh by a further male medical fantasy of surgically fashioning a male body into a female one. These fantasies are based in the male imagination, not in any female reality. It is this female reality that the surgically-constructed woman does not possess, not because women innately carry some essence of femininity but because these men have not had to live in a female body with all the history that entails. It is that history that is basic

to female reality, and yes, history is based to a certain extent on female biology (Raymond xx).
22. "In transsexualism, males put on "female" bodies (which are in fact pseudofemale). In a real sense they are separated from their original mothers by the rituals of the counseling process. . . . These "patients" are reborn from males. . . . The surgeons and hormone therapists of the transsexual kingdom, in their effort to give birth, can be said to produce feminine persons. They cannot produce women" (Daly: 68).
23. Also see Butler 2006; Chase; Felski; Koyama; Lane; Prosser 1998, 2006; Shepherdson; Whittle.
24. There are academic supports for this philosophical program (for example, Salomonsen) and it does generate its own rigorous critical tradition of Ecofeminism (Gaard & Gruen; Keller; Warren). For the history of Indian tantra, see Wedemeyer.
25. Thalia Mae Bettcher calls these two camps "Transgender Model" and "the Wrong Body Model." The former is favored by most of what is now called Queer Theory because of the agency it assumes trans people have to construct and define themselves. The most influential representative of this attitude is Judith Butler (1990). The "Wrong Body Model" is represented by Jay Prosser (1998).
26. Bettcher writes that the work of C. Jacob Hale represents "a kind of intervention in these borderland disputes" (2014), adding nuance to the ever-growing discourse.
27. Known in philosophy as Descartes' *cogito*—as in, "*Cogito ergo sum*" *("I think, therefore I am")*, his famous conclusion about the irreducibility of the subject. We can throw the entire objective world into doubt, to the point that we are convinced the entire objective world is an illusion, but what always remains is an observing self-awareness. Descartes theorized that this subjectivity was an entirely different substance than the material, objective world. Modern theorists have tried to reconcile this dualism by grounding the undeniable self in the material of the body.
28. Cited in Salamon p. 36.
29. These are the eye, ear, nose, tongue, body, and mind, which synthesize the senses and gives rise to feelings (i.e., reactions) and volitions.
30. "The mental states responsible for bodily and mental activity, for example, hunger, attentiveness" (Siderits 36).
31. Kalupahana 71.
32. Siderits defines consciousness as "the awareness of mental states" (36).
33. See Siderits (37) for a traditional Buddhist exegesis of this point.
34. See especially Chapter 13, "Homogenizing Versus Holistic Views of Gender and Sexuality"
35. Michel Onfray (2015) accounts for this in his philosophical system, arguing that the practice of philosophy—that is, the effort to *live philosophically*—can be part of a *neuronal training*, so that what may previously have been assumed to be a mere intellectual activity actually has felt, embodied, material effects. A synthesis of the science here is in Daniel Siegel 2015.
36. There are countless books about this theory. For example: Buescher; Newland; The Cowherds; Tsering.
37. See Deurlinger: 36 for a discussion of conventional and ultimate "persons."

CHAPTER THREE

1. Sex-confirmation surgery used to be called "sexual-reassignment surgery" (SRS) or a "sex change." "Sex-confirmation surgery" is now preferred since it does not connote that the person's sex ever needed to change—they were already what they were, and the surgery only outwardly confirms that. A less laden term is simply "bottom surgery."
2. A subject of much of Stone 2006.
3. Or even dogmatically top or bottom gay men, for that matter.
4. On "stealth" see Cooke; Ira; Newbury; Roberts 2009, 2013; St. James Williams.
5. https://thatguykas.wordpress.com/2015/11/14/living-stealth-a-guest-blogger-and-his-choice-to-remain-secretly-trans/
6. http://www.advocate.com/politics/transgender/2015/04/15/after-years-hiding-hollywood-trans-actress-trace-lysette-finally-liv
7. For the story of the murder of Barry Winchell for his transamory, see Addams.
8. Space does not allow for a lengthy analysis of a wide range of published accounts, but I would include here works by Andrews, Bono, Finney-Boylan, Hill, Jacques, Jennings, Krieger, Mock, Serano, and others cited in this book.
9. On the relationship between geometry and aesthetics, see Henderson ch. 3; Leyton; Rawes.
10. A note of thanks to Ziggy Snow for helping me articulate this point.
11. For a few other examples, Katie Rain Hill writes, "After years of experiencing shame and hatred of my body, it was an amazing feeling to finally have the right part down there. Not to mention, I could now flirt with guys and know that if something ever happened between us, I wouldn't have to awkwardly explain why I had a penis between my legs" (Hill ch. 2). Bono writes, "My breasts had been in my way since they first appeared, and now they made me uncomfortable, even embarrassed, during sex. I found myself mentally checking out or squirming when my breasts were touched, wanting to leave my body completely. This surgery felt like a great step toward becoming more comfortable in my body" (Bono ch. 5). And Andrews: "None of us were taught to have shame about our bodies, yet I still felt it. I wished I could stand up and just pee wherever I wanted when we were playing outside, like my cousin Dewayne did" (Andrews ch. 3).
12. Serano 2013: chapter 10.
13. Jurinski
14. George Yancey, *Dehumanizing Christians: Cultural Competition in a Multicultural World*. Piscataway: Transaction Publishers, 2013.
15. This point was made by Stone as a spur to trans self-reflection, and is made as a condemnation by Daly, Raymond, Jeffreys and other Trans Exclusive Radical Feminists. For an analysis of Stone's views, see Bettcher 2006:193.
16. For an excellent collection of aggressively critical essays about "gender-systems" see Sycamore, Matt Bernstein (2010-01-08). *Nobody Passes: Rejecting the Rules of Gender and Conformity* (p. 9). The introduction, Mathilda writes, "In a pass/fail situation, standards for acceptance may vary, but somebody always gets trampled. I wanted to challenge all standards of authenticity, to confront societal mores and countercultural norms. Instead of policing the borders with pass/fail politics, I was intent on confronting the perilous intersections of identity, categorization, and community in order to challenge the very notion of belonging."

17. An example of this ethos is Jen Richards' piece "No Wrong Way." It is admittedly more ecumenical than what I have argued for here, but I would not object if the attitude she conveys prevailed. (http://smartassjen.com/no-wrong-way/)

CHAPTER FOUR
1. Stafford.
2. Kellaway and Brydum.
3. http://www.advocate.com/transgender/2016/9/12/these-are-trans-people-killed-2016
4. Santos.
5. "If there is no such thing today as femininity, it is because there never was"(de Beauvoir 4).
6. Hernandez and Locke.
7. Brunnhölzl.
8. Molloy.
9. The judge in the case of Jennifer Laude's murder included in her ruling that "The mitigating circumstance of passion and obfuscation is present in this case" (Talusan).
10. Dennis.
11. Liljas.
12. Brydum.
13. Abdullah; Eagle. The U.K. has a similar statute that requires trans people to disclose their trans status to prior to any act of physical intimacy (Lees 2013; O'Connell).
14. For more trans women's accounts see Jen Richard's TV series *Her Story;* Cayne; Corazón; Daniari; Hill; Kohner; Mock; Neyfack; O'Toole; Reid 2016*b*; Tannehill; Willis etc.
15. See Serano 2007, chapter 2.
16. This famously came up in interviews between Laverne Cox and Katie Couric (McDonough) and Janet Mock and Piers Morgan; see Molloy 2015.
17. Tourjee 2015.
18. Serano writes, "Media depictions of trans women, whether they take the form of characters or actual people, usually fall under one of two main archetypes: the 'deceptive transsexual' or the 'pathetic transsexual'" (2007: ch. 2).
19. http://www.nationalreview.com/article/356501/bradley-manning-not-woman-kevin-d-williamson
20. http://www.nationalreview.com/379188/laverne-cox-not-woman
21. For a criticism that overlaps imperfectly with mine, see Mark Joseph Stern in *Slate* (June 3, 2014). http://www.slate.com/blogs/outward/2014/06/03/kevin_williamson_shows_us_to_dehumanize_a_trans_person_in_three_simple_steps.html
22. For example, the South African runner Caster Semenya who was nearly stripped of her Olympic medals over her chromosomes that did not fit into the absolute binary chromosomal model; see Longman.
23. Laqueur writes, "For two millennia the ovary, an organ that had by the early nineteenth century become a synecdoche for woman, had not even a name of its own. Galen (129-c.200 C.E.) refers to it by the same word he uses for the

male testes, *orchesis*, allowing context to make clear which sex he is concerned with" (4).
24. *Politics* 1260a
25. (Aristotle. *Generation of Animals* 2.4.738b20-23)
26. Laqueur notes how the ancients "saw no need to develop a precise vocabulary of genital anatomy because if the female body was a less hot, less perfect, and hence less potent version of the canonical body, then distinct organic, much less genital, landmarks matter far less than the metaphysical hierarchies they illustrated" (35).
27. See Reeve.
28. Williamson 2013.
29. In this important essay, Sontag discusses the tendency to interpret illness as metaphor for a deep teleological meaning. When she was diagnosed with cancer, she noticed her own doctors speaking of cancer as a kind of anthropomorphic, pernicious force, insinuating that she, as the patient, had some moral relationship to her illness. Confronted with this, she delves into the history of cancer discourse, exposing the illness's long association with psychological repression read as spiritual failure. Cancer, she notices, is not the only illness with such a rich milieu. She compares cancer *qua* spiritual failure to tuberculosis, which was long associated with another kind of spiritual failure—that of melancholic, artistic self-indulgence. In her 1989 companion piece, *AIDS and Its Metaphors,* she analyzes the way the illness is embedded in a new discourse colored by military metaphors. In all three cases, these metaphors have nothing to do with science. Rather, they reflect our impulse to read reality in terms of its hidden, moral telos—a mere illusion that exacerbates the material suffering of illness.
30. Jones, S. 2003; Sykes; Venter
31. "Chromosomes are only one form of sex-determining mechanism in the natural world. Birds have sex chromosomes, but the system is the reverse of mammals. . . . " and the list of biological variations go on. (Richardson 6). Moreover, whatever we might call biological sex "is the result of a choreography of genes, hormones, gonads, genitals, and secondary sex characteristics" (8).
32. See Padawer. Williamson did not foresee the Olympic Committee finally allowing transgender athletes, including U.S. cyclist Chris Mosier, to officially compete in January 2016; see Steele.
33. "Sex chromosomes evolved as a sex-determining mechanism; they carry a critical switch in a larger pathway of genes that determine sex. That the X and Y carry the key genes involved in the characteristic sexual dimorphism of a species, however, is dubious. We know that genes with sex-specific fitness effects need not be located on the sex chromosomes. . . . We also know that extreme sexual dimorphism is observed in many species that lack sex chromosomes. Thus, sexual dimorphism may be reliably transmitted without a genotopic dimorphism such as sex chromosomes" (Richardson 204).
34. Geertz relayed a famous anecdote: "There is an Indian story—at least I heard it as an Indian story—about an Englishman who, having been told that the world rested on a platform which rested on the back of an elephant which rested in turn on the back of a turtle, asked (perhaps he was an ethnographer, it is the way they behave), what did the turtle rest on? Another turtle? And that turtle? "Ah, Sahib, after that it is turtles all the way down" (Geertz 29).

CHAPTER FIVE

1. Sontag writes, "What situation could prompt this curious project for transforming a text? History gives us the materials for an answer. Interpretation first appears in the culture of late classical antiquity, when the power and credibility of myth had been broken by the 'realistic' view of world introduced by scientific enlightenment. Once the question that haunts post-mythic consciousness—that of the seemliness of religious symbols—had been asked, the ancient texts were in their pristine form no longer acceptable. Then interpretation was summoned, to reconcile the ancient texts to 'modern' demands" (3).
2. Bettcher 2014a: 392.
3. "Both the myth about TB and the current myth about cancer propose that one is responsible for one's disease. But the cancer imagery is far more punishing. Given the romantic values in use for judging character and disease, some glamour attaches to having a disease thought to come from being too full of passion. But there is mostly shame attached to a disease thought to stem from the repression of emotion. . . . The view of cancer as a disease of the failure of expressiveness condemns the cancer patient: expresses pity but also conveys contempt.... The tubercular could be an outlaw or a misfit; the cancer personality is regarded more simply, and with condescension, as one of life's losers" (Sontag, *Illness as Metaphor*: 48-49).
4. Michel Onfray writes that the notion of "desire as lack" assumes that men and women "proceed from a primitive unity split up by the gods as punishment for their insolent enjoyment of perfect totality. Pleasure is defined as the fantastic perfection of the spherical, complete animal. Desire-as-lack, and pleasure that fills this lack, are the cause of uneasiness and sexual wretchedness . . . In effect, this dangerous fiction leads most people to search for the nonexistent, so they find nothing but frustration. The quest for Prince Charming or its female equivalent produces deceptions: the real never compares to the ideal. Wanting fullness inevitably leads to the sadness of incompleteness . . . We stop fooling ourselves the day we index what is real to us to what is imaginary . . . desire is not lack. It is excess on the verge of bursting. Pleasure is not the specious realization of completeness; it is the conjuration of an effusive overflow" (Onfray 41-42).
5. Wittgenstein §581: "An expectation is embedded in a situation, from which it arises."
6. See Bersani and Kemp.
7. An extensive treatment is in Bataille.
8. Female to male, a.k.a., trans male, transman, etc. Hale prefers not to capitalize the acronym.

CHAPTER SIX

1. In *Assuming a Body*, Gayle Salamon also defends the usefulness of Merleau-Ponty: "There is something enabling in this philosophy of ambiguity; it is precisely the ambiguity attending sexuality that can become the means for understanding bodies, lives, and especially *relationality* outside the domains of male and female" (44).
2. Serano 2007, chapters 5 and 6.
3. Mase III; Michaels; Pittman.

4. Here, I am aware of the tensions produced when emphasizing sexuality or erotics in trans discourse. It suffices to reproduce Salamon's sound thoughts on the matter:

> There is danger of overstating the confluence of sexuality and identity, and this danger is particularly acute in relations to transpeople. Second-wave feminist receptions of transsexuality, some recent biological theories about transsexuality, and popular misconceptions of transsexuality all share this conflation of gender expression with sexual expression. Historically, transsexuality has often been fantasized to be—and thus described as—a kind of hypersexualization; some trans writers' effort to disengage from the realm of sexuality stems from this historical conflation of transgenderism with sexuality. . . . But deemphasizing sexuality to avoid the perils of fetishization would seem to be accompanied by a different set of perils, for it is certainly an impoverished account of subjectivity that cannot make room for desire, and we might ask what sorts of contortions result when trans subjects are required to suppress or deny their sexuality. Might there be a way of avoiding the groundless conflation of transsexuality with sexual fetishism without denying trans subjects a sexuality altogether? Is there room in this picture for desire? (Salamon 45)

5. Salamon observes that "Merleau-Ponty begins with a body, vaguely defined, and then moves to a consideration of the sexual schema beneath it, only after which the physiognomy of the sexual regions of the body become delineated. It is only after that delineation wrought by desire that gender appears, first as a bodily fact ("the masculine body") and finally as an emotional one. . . . The sexual schema is. . . *strictly individual*" (Salamon 48).
6. It seems to only be treated as a polysemous organ by gay male writers like Bersani, Dean, and Kemp. When straight male writers like Battaille, Freud, and Lacan address it, it always represents death, darkness, negation, abjection, etc. The same associations have been made by female writers speculating on male sexuality, such as Iragaray and Kristeva (Thomas 38, 68, 70, 79, 82-83, 92, 109).
7. Almost all straight cis male transam accounts have been very brief and, probably for fear of being perceived as fetishizers, never do the subjects address their or their lovers' bodies with much specificity (with the possible exception of Freel, who produces very conventional and problematic heteronormative tropes).
8. The details of the instrument are not essential. Salamon comments:

> . . . desire . . . is embodied but—importantly—not located. When Merleau-Ponty writes, "From the part of the body which it especially occupies, sexuality spreads forth," this may be read as something other than a phallic reference veiled by some coyness that forbids his naming the part. There is an important ambiguity secured with Merleau-Ponty's refusal to name the penis as an encampment of sexuality, an ambiguity that performs an unyoking of bodily parts from bodily pleasures. The join between desire and the body is the location of sexuality, and that join may be a penis, or some other phallus, or some other body part, or a region of the body that is not individuated into a part, or a bodily auxiliary that is not organically

attached to the body. This passage asserts that the most important aspect of sexuality is not any particular part—not even the behavior of that part—but the "general function" which causes that part to be animated, the means through which it is brought into my bodily sense of myself and is incorporated into my self-understanding through a reaching out toward the world (51).

CHAPTER SEVEN

1. In this section I will speak specifically about straight cis male transamory, though the work of Tompkins suggests that much of it translates to straight cis female transamory.
2. On bottom shaming, see Johnson, Lowder, Michael, Moore, and Rodriguez-Jimenez. On the history and content of stereotypes about women and men's sexuality, see Beauvoir, Dean, Kemp, and Thomas.
3. As Leo Bersani notes in his essay "Is the Rectum a Grave?" "The only 'honorable' sexual behavior consists in being active, in dominating, in penetrating, and in thereby exercising one's authority" (19).
4. http://thecasualsexproject.com/about/
5. Bussell; Nal & Gotter.

WORKS CITED

Abdullah, Mina. "Why America's Call for LGBTQ Rights is Insecure." *Berkeley Political Review,* November 10, 2014.

Addams, Calpernia. "Soldier's Girl - The Reality." *Calpernia.*

Adler, Dahlia. "A QUILTBAG YA/NA Compendium." *The Daily Dahlia* (blog), February 19, 2014.

Ailith, L'lerrét Jazelle. "From The Black Trans Girls Who Shut It Down." *L'lerrét,* January 22, 2016.

Alder, David. "A Rose by Any Other Name." *The Queer Oral History Project* (blog), March 27, 2014.

Allen, Emma. "Unpacking Transphobia." *Radical Women,* June 2013.

Anders, Sari M. "Beyond masculinity: Testosterone, Gender/Sex, and Human Social Behavior in a Comparative Context." *Frontiers in Neuroendocrinology* 34, no. 3 (2013): 198-210.

Anderson, Carol. *Pain and Its Ending: The Four Noble Truths in the Therav da Buddhist Canon.* New York: Routledge, 2013.

Anderson-Minshall, Diane. "My Attraction to Trans People Is Not a Fetish." *The Advocate Magazine,* October 2, 2013.

Anderson-Minshall, Jacob. "My Wife is a Trans Am." *The Advocate Magazine,* October 14, 2013.

—. "Being Married to a Lesbian Doesn't Make Me Less of a Man." *The Advocate Magazine,* July 1, 2013.

Andrews, Arin. *Some Assembly Required: The Not-So-Secret Life of a Transgender Teen.* New York: Simon and Schuster, 2014.

Aristotle. *Politics.* Indianapolis: Hackett, 1998.

Aylesworth, Gary. "Postmodernism." *The Stanford Encyclopedia of Philosophy,* Edited by Edward N. Zalta, 2015.

Baldwin, James. "On Being "White" And Other Lies." In *Black on White,* Edited by David R. Roediger. New York: Schocken Books, 1998. Originally Published in *Essence Magazine,* 1984.

Bataille, Georges. *Erotism: Death and Sensuality.* Berkeley: City Lights Publishers, 1986.

Beauvoir, Simone de. *The Second Sex.* Translated by Constance Borde and Sheila Malovany-Chevallier. New York: Vintage, 2011.

Belaswki, Sarah E, and Carey Jean Sojka. "Intimate Relationships." In *Trans Bodies, Trans Selves: A Resource for the Transgender Community,* Edited by Erickson-Schroth. Oxford: Oxford University Press, 2014.

Bentham, Jeremy. *The Works of Jeremy Bentham,* vol 4 (1843), Edited by John Bowring. Edinburgh: William Tait, 2016.

Bersani, Leo. *Is the Rectum a Grave?: and Other Essays.* Chicago: University of Chicago Press, 2009.

Bettcher, Thalia Mae. "Other-Worldly Philosophy." *Philosopher* (blog), August 16, 2015.

——. "Intersexuality, Transsexuality, Transgender." In *Oxford Handbook of Feminist Theory*, Edited by Mary Hawkesworth and Lisa Jane Disch. Oxford: Oxford University Press, 2015.

——. "Trapped in the Wrong Theory: Re-Thinking Trans Oppression and Resistance." *Journal of Women in Culture and Society* 39, no. 2 (2014): 383-403.

——. "When Selves Have Sex: What the Phenomenology of Trans Sexuality Can Teach Us About Sexual Orientation." *Journal of Homosexuality* 61, no. 5 (2014): 605-620.

——. "Transphobia." *Transgender Studies Quarterly* "Postposttranssexual Terms for a 21st Century" 1, no.1 (2014), 249-251.

——. "Trans Women and Interpretive Intimacy: Some Initial Reflections." In *The Essential Handbook of Women's Sexuality*, Edited by . D. Castenada, 51-68. California: Praeger, 2013.

——. "Feminist Perspectives on Trans Issues," *The Stanford Encyclopedia of Philosophy*, Edited by Edward N. Zalta (2009/2014).

——. "Trans Women and the Meaning of 'Woman'." In *Philosophy of Sex: Contemporary Readings*, Edited by A. Soble, N. Power and R. Halwani, 233-250. Maryland: Rowman & Littlefield, 2012.

——. "Full-Frontal Morality: The Naked Truth about Gender." *Hypatia: A Journal of Feminist Philosophy* 27, no. 2 (2012): 319-337.

——. "Evil Deceivers and Make-Believers: Transphobic Violence and the Politics of Illusion." *Hypatia: A Journal of Feminist Philosophy* 22, no.3 (2007): 43-65.

——. "Appearance, Reality and Gender Deception: Reflections on Transphobic Violence and the Politics of Pretense." in *Violence, Victims, and Justifications*, Felix Ó Murchadha ed. Oxford:
Peter Lang Ltd, International Academic Publishers, 2006.

Biko, Cherno. "Hurt People Protest: Black Lives Matter at Creating Change 2016." *Medium*, January 30, 2016.

Bodhi, Bikku. *In the Buddha's Words: An Anthology of Discourses from the Pali Canon.* Somerville: Wisdom Publications, 2005.

Boellstorff, Tom et al. "Decolonizing Transgender." Duke University Press: *Transgender Studies Quarterly* 1, no.1 (2014): 419-439.

Bono, Chaz. *Transition: The Story of How I Became a Man.* New York: Dutton, 2011.

Boyd, Helen. *She's Not the Man I Married: My Life with a Transgender Husband.* Berkeley: Seal, 2007.

——. "Love & Shame & Having a Thing for Trans Women." *En /Gender: Helen Boyd's Journal of Gender & Trans Issues*, September 17, 2013.

Brown, Curt. "Friend: Never saw signs of violence by Joseph Pemberton; calls New Bedford Marine on trial in Philippines 'peaceful individual'." *South Coast Today*, March 30, 2015.

Brownstone, Sydney. "New Report Highlights Police Hostility Toward Transgender Women of Color." *The Village Voice,* June 4, 2013.

Bryant, Levi. "Five Darwinian/Posthumanist Theses." *Larval Subjects* (blog), April 2, 2012.

Brydum, Sunnivie. "Marine Claims 'Trans Panic' in Murder of Trans Filipina Jennifer Laude." *Advocate,* August 24, 2015.

Brunnhölzl, Karl. *The Heart Attack Sutra.* Ithaca: Snow Lion, 2012.

Buescher, John B. *Echoes from an Empty Sky: The Origin of the Buddhist Doctrine of the Two Truths.* Ithaca: Snow Lion, 2005.

Bussell, Rachel Kramer. "Why Do So Many Younger Men Have Erectile Dysfunction?" *Mic,* October 27, 2015.

Butler, Judith. *Bodies That Matter: On the Discursive Limits of Sex.* New York: Routledge, 1993.

—. *Gender Trouble: Feminism and the Subversion of Identity.* New York: Routledge, 1990.

—. "Doing Justice to Someone: Sex Reassignment and Allegories of Transsexuality." In *The Transgender Studies Reader,* Edited by Susan Stryker and Stephen Whittle. New York: Taylor & Francis, 2006.

—. *Giving an Account of Oneself.* New York: Fordham University Press, 2005.

Cayne, Candis. "Candis Cayne on the 'Obstacles' of Dating as a Trans Woman." *E NEWS,* March 21, 2016.

Chagdud Rinpoche. "Thirty Seven Points of Practice." *Chagdud Gonpa Brazil.*

Chandra, Navamita. "Bullies In the City: Molestation & More." *Express Magazine,* July 26, 2016.

Chase, Cheryl. "Hermaphrodites with Attitude: Mapping the Emergence of Intersex Political Activism." In *The Transgender Studies Reader,* Edited by Susan Stryker and Stephen Whittle. New York: Taylor & Francis, 2006.

Chogye Trichen. *Parting from the Four Attachments.* Ithaca: Snow Lion, 2003.

Coates, Ta-Nehisi. *Between the World and Me.* New york: Spiegel & Grau, 2015.

Conway, Lynn. "The Many Shades of 'Out'." *The Huffington Post,* February 2, 2016.

Cooke, Suzan. "The Many Shades of Stealth." *TransAdvocate,* 2013.

Corazon, Alexa. "The Real Struggle Behind Trans Dating." *Huffington Post,* June 9, 2016.

Cox, Laverne. "Laverne Cox of OITNB Talks About How Men Who Love Transgender Women Are Stigmatized. (SiriusXM Interview)." SoundCloud audio, 0:44, September 2015.

—. "Laverne Cox at Creating Change 2014." YouTube video, 30:46, February 5, 2014.

Crosby, Richard A., and Nicole L. Pitts. "Caught Between Different Worlds: How Transgendered Women May Be "Forced" Into Risky Sex." *Journal of Sex Research* 44, no.1 (2007): 43-48.

Cruz, Carmen. "Straight men now feel the need to say 'no homo' when discussing emotions." *The Guardian,* February 23, 2014.

Dalai Lama. *Stages of Meditation*. Ithaca: Snow Lion, 2003.

Daniari, Serena. "What Happened When I Revealed to Men on Tinder That I'm a Transgender Woman." *Cambio*, September 17, 2015.

Daoud, Sarah. "To BYP and the larger community of Chicago Activists." *Tired Sista* (blog), December 21, 2015.

Darwin, Charles. "Letter no. 2814." Darwin Correspondence Project. Accessed September 20, 2016.

Dawes, Piper. "New Word: Transamory." *pipertalks.tumblr.* (blog), January 29, 2013.

Deam, Tim. *Unlimited Intimacy: Reflections on the Subculture of Barebacking*. Chicago: University of Chicago Press, 2009.

Delgado, Richard. *Whiteness: A Critical Reader*. Philadelphia: Temple University Press, 1997.

Dennis, Rob and Paul Burgarino. "Witness relates brutal slaying." *Oakland Tribune*, 8 June 2005.

Deurlinger, James. *Indian Buddhist Theories of Persons: Vasubandhu's Refutation of the Theory of a Self*. New York: Routledge, 2003.

Dolan, Zoe. *Transgender No More*. Amazon Digital Services, 2015.

Doniger, Wendy. *The Laws of Manu*. New York: Penguin, 1992.

Dotson, Kristie. "How is this Paper Philosophy?." *Comparative Philosophy* 3, no. 1 (2012): 3-29.

Duerlinger, James. *Indian Buddhist Theories of Persons: Vasubandhu's Refutation of the Theory of a Self*. London: Routledge Curzon, 2003.

Eagle, Tyler. "States need to outlaw gay, trans panic defenses." *The Columbia Chronicle*, October 6, 2014.

Eazy-E. *Nobody Move*. In *Eazy-Duz-It*. Ruthless & Priority Records, 1988.

Edison, Avery. "I'm Trans and on Tinder, but I am not a fetish for your sexual bucket list." *The Guardian*, December 12, 2014.

Eisner, Shiri. *Bi: Notes for a Bisexual Revolution*. Berkeley: Seal Press, 2013. Kindle Edition.

Emmanuel, Steven M. *A Companion to Buddhist Philosophy*. Hoboken: Wiley-Blackwell, 2013.

Erickson-Schroth, Laura. *Trans Bodies, Trans Selves: A Resource for the Transgender Community*. New York: Oxford University Press, 2014.

Fairchild, Phaylen. "The Sad Life of the Trans Attracted Man." *Phaylen online* (blog), March 27, 2016.

Fausto-Sterling, Anne. *Sexing the Body: Gender Politics and the Construction of Sexuality*. New York: Basic Books, 2000.

Felski, Rita. "Fin de siècle, Fin du Sexe: Transsexuality, Postmodernism, and the Death of History." In *The Transgender Studies Reader*, Edited by Susan Stryker and Stephen Whittle. New York: Taylor & Francis, 2006.

Finch, Sam Dylan. "8 Tips on Respectfully Talking Pleasure, Sex, and Bodies With your Trans Lover." *everyday feminism*, December 16, 2014.

Finney-Boylan, Jennifer. *She's Not There: A Life in Two Genders*. New York: Broadway Books, 2013.

—. *I'm Looking Through You: Growing Up Haunted: A Memoir.* New York: Broadway Books, 2008.

Firestone, Shulamith. *The Dialectic of Sex: The Case for Feminist Revolution.* New York: Farrar, Straus and Giroux, 2003.

Fischer, Nancy L, and Steven Seidman eds. *Introducing New Sexuality Studies.* New York: Routledge, 2011.

Flory, Tracy-Clark. "What's behind transexual attraction?" *Salon,* October 21, 2011.

Freel, Michael David. *Trans-Oriented: A Guide to Love and Relationships for Men who Love Transsexual Women.* Victoria: Friesen Press, 2016.

Friedan, Betty. *The Feminine Mystique.* New York: Norton, 2001.

Futurum, Torraine. "The 3 Types of People You Meet As A Trans Person On OKCupid." *Huffington Post,* September 19, 2015.

Gaard, Greta and Lori Gruen. "Ecofeminism: Toward global justice and planetary health." *Society and Nature* 2, no.1 (1993), 1-35.

Gampopa. *The Jewel Ornament of Liberation.* Khenpo Kopnchog Gyaltsen Rinpoche trans. Ithaca: Snow Lion, 1998.

Giaimo, Cara. "More Than Words: Queer, Part 1 (The Early Years)." *AutoStraddle* (blog), January 9, 2013.

—. "More Than Words: Queer, Part 2 (Growing Pains)." *AutoStraddle* (blog), February 5, 2013

Giovanniello, Sarah. "NCAVP report: 2012 hate violence disproportionately target transgender women of color." *Glaad,* June 4, 2013.

Girshik, Lori B. *Transgender Voices: Beyond Women and Men.* Lebanon: University Press of New England, 2008.

Gouges, Olympe de. "Déclaration des Droits de la Femme et de la Citoyenne." Amazon Digital Services, Kindle edition, 2016.

Graham, David A. "A Federal Judge's Ruling Against North Carolina's HB2." *The Atlantic,* August 26, 2016.

Green, Chris. "'Cisgender' has been added to the Oxford English Dictionary." *Independent Magazine,* June 25, 2015.

Greenblatt, Stephen. *The Swerve: How the World Became Modern.* New York: Norton, 2011.

Griffin, Wendy. *Daughters of the Goddess: Studies of Identity, Healing, and Empowerment.* Lanham: Altamira Press, 1999.

Gross, Rita. *Buddhism After Patriarchy.* Albany: SUNY Press, 1992.

Gruber, Perry. "About the Transamorous Network." Accessed September 23, 2016.

—. "I Like Trans-Am." *The Transamorous Network* (blog). Accessed September 23, 2016.

Grynbaum, Michael M. "Mayor de Blasio Is Set to Ease Rules on Circumcision Ritual." *The New York Times,* February 24, 2015.

Gubb, Sophia. "Why Attraction to Trans People Is Not A 'Taste'." *SophiaGubb,* July 26, 2014.

—. "Family In A Feminist World." *Sophia Gubbs* (blog), August 27, 2016.

—. "'I'm A Man And I'm With A Trans Woman, Does That Make Me Gay Or Straight?' (Or 'Bi?')." *Sophia Gubbs* (blog), October 1, 2013.

Halberstam, Judith. *In a Queer Time and Place: Transgender Bodies, Subcultural Lives.* New York: New York University Press, 2005.

Hale, C Jacob. "Leatherdyke Boys and Their Daddies: How to Have Sex without Women or Men." *Social Text* 15, no. 3 and 4 (Fall/Winter 1997 1997): 223-36.

—. "Suggested Rules for Non-Transsexuals Writing about Transsexuals, Transsexuality, Transsexualism, or Trans___." http://sandystone.com/hale.rules.html.

Hamblin, James. "Toxic Masculinity and Murder." *Salon,* June 16, 2016.

Hanson, Amanda Gernentz. "The Transgender Murder Crisis: Why Were There So Many Killings in 2015?" *Law Street Media,* January 22, 2016.

Harmony, Princess. "People Who Fetishize Trans Women Are Not Allies." *The Establishment,* July 18, 2016.

Harper, Susan. "Not My Goddess, Not My Feminism, Not My Priestesses." *Witches and Pagans,* October 9, 2016.

Harvey, Peter. *An Introduction to Buddhism.* Cambridge: Cambridge University Press, 2012.

Hegel, G.W.F. *Lectures on the Philosophy of World History.* Translated by H.B. Nisbet. Cambridge: Cambridge University Press, 1981.

Henderson, David and Daina Taimina. *Experiencing Geometry.* New York: Pearson Education, 2004.

Hernandez, G. "Bittersweet justice: in the wake of the Gwen Araujo trial, activists are grimly aware of how difficult it is to obtain a first-degree murder conviction when the victim is transgender." *The Advocate,* 22 November 2005.

Hill, Katie Rain. *Rethinking Normal: A Memoir in Transition.* New York: Simon & Schuster, 2014.

Holloway, Kali. "Toxic masculinity is killing men: The roots of male trauma." *Salone,* June 12, 2015.

Hooks, Bell. *Feminism Is For Everybody.* Cambridge: South End Press, 2000.

Hsu, Kevin J. et al. "Who are gynandromorphophilic men? Characterizing men with sexual interest in transgender women." *Psychological Medicine* 46, no.4 (2015): 1-9.

Hume, David. *A Treatise of Human Nature.* Oxford: Oxford University Press, 2000.

Hung Angels. HungAngels.com

Ira, Stephan. "Stealth Shaming: What It Is, Why You Shouldn't Do It, and How Not To." *Super-Matteachine.wordpress* (blog), September 14, 2011.

Jacques, Juliet. *Trans: A Memoir.* London: Verso, 2015.

—. "On the 'dispute' between radical feminism and trans people." *New Statesman,* August 6, 2014.

Jakubowski, Kaylee. "How to Respectfully Love a Trans Woman: Navigating Transmisogyny in Your Romantic Relationship." *everyday feminism,* January 19, 2015.

Jeffreys, Sheila. *Gender Hurts: A Feminist Analysis of the Politics of Transgenderism.* New York: Routledge, 2014.

Jennings, Jazz. *Being Jazz: My Life as a Transgender Teen*. New York: Random House, 2016

Johnson, Ramon. "You Could Be Bottom Shaing (And Not Even Know It)." *About Relationships (Gaylife.About.Com)*.

Jones, Kelsie Brynn. "Trans-Exclusionary Radical Feminism: What Exactly Is It, And Why Does It Hurt?" *Huffington Post*, February 2, 2016.

Jones, Lana de Holanda. "How Many More Transgender Murders Will Take PLace in Brazil?" *The Huffington Post*, April 08, 2016.

Jones, Steve. *Y: The Descent of Men*. New York: Houghton Mifflin Harcourt, 2003.

Jurinski, James John. *Religion on Trial: A Handbook with Cases, Laws, and Documents*. Santa Barbara: ABC-CLIO, 2003.

Kacere, Laura. "Transmisogyny 101: What It Is and What Can We Do About It." *everyday feminism*, January 27, 2014.

Kalupahana, David. *A History of Buddhist Philosophy*. Honolulu: University of Hawaii Press, 1992.

Kapali, Rukshana. "About men who are attracted to transwomen." *Pahichan*.

Kappel, Aaron. "Trans-Exclusionary Feminists Cannot Exclude My Humanity." *The Establishment*, December 8, 2015.

—. "Let Transgender People Speak for Themselves." *The Establishment*, January 5, 2016.

Kellaway, Mitch. "After Years of Hiding in Hollywood, Trans Actress Trace Lysette Is Finally 'Living Out Loud'." *The Advocate*, April 15, 2015.

Kellaway, Mitch and Sunnivie Brydum. "The 21 Trans Women Killed in 2015." *The Advocate*, January 12, 2016.

Keller, Catherine. "Dark Vibrations: ecofeminism and the democracy of creation." *Annual Howard Harrod/CRSC Lecture at Vanderbilt*, April 6, 2005.

Keown, Damian. *Buddhism: A Very Short Introduction*. Oxford: Oxford University Press, 2013.

Kemp, Jonathan. *The Penetrated Male*. New York: Punctum, 2013.

Klein, Fritz. *The Bisexual Option*. New York: Routledge, 2014.

Kohner, Claire-Renee. "I Created Dating Profiles As A Transgender Woman And As The Person I was Before Transition, and I learned a Lot About Finding Love as a Lady." *Bustle*, May 14, 2015.

Koyama, Emi. "Whose Feminism Is It Anyway?: The Unspoken Racism of the Trans Inclusion Debate." In *The Transgender Studies Reader*, Edited by Susan Stryker and Stephen Whittle. New York: Taylor & Francis, 2006.

Lane, Riki. "Trans as Bodily Becoming: Rethinking the Biological as Diversity, Not Dichotomy." *Hypatia* 24, no.3 (Summer 2009):136-157.

Laqueur, Thomas. *Making Sex: Body and Gender from the Greeks to Freud*. Cambridge: Harvard University Press, 1992.

Lee, Sadie. "Final Call: Kate Bornstein." *Diva Magazine* 125, (2006):114.

Lees, Paris. "My Adventures Using Tinder as a Trans Woman." *Vice*, May 28, 2015.

———. "Stop Media Lies About Transgender Kids." *Vice*, May 22, 2014.

———. "Should Trans People Have to Disclose Their Birth Gender Before Sex?" *Vice*, July 1, 2013.

———. "The Trans vs. Radical Feminist Twitter War Is Making Me Sick." *Vice*, August 21, 2014.

———. "The Vice Guide to Being Trans." *Vice*, October 31, 2012.

Lenning, Emily. "*This journey is not for the faint of heart: An investigation of challenges facing transgender individuals and their significant others.*" PhD dissertation, Western Michigan University, 2008.

Levine, Hillary Lauren. "Trans People and Their Partners Talk About Their Relationships." Buzzfeed video, 2:30. August 18, 2015.

Leyton, Michael. "The Foundations of Aesthetics." In *Aesthetic Computing*, Edited by Paul Fishwick, 289-313. Boston: MIT Press, 2006.

Liljas, Per. "Philippine Transgender Murder Becomes a Rallying Point for LGBT Rights." *Time*, October 24, 2014.

Locke, M. " Defence lawyers claim heat of passion in transgender killing case.'" *Associated Press*, 3 June 2004.

Longman, Jeré. "Understanding the Controversy Over Caster Semenya." *New York Times*, August 18, 2016.

Lovaas, Karen. *LGBT Studies and Queer Theory: New Conflict, Collaborations, and Contested Terrain*. New York: Routledge, 2013.

Lowder, Bryan J. "What's With All the Bottom Shaming in *How to Get Away With Murder*?" *Slate*, October 28, 2014.

Maclay, Tyler. "No More Exclusion, Let's Talk Solution." *Things Feminist Will Understand* (blog), February 13, 2015.

MacMillen, Hayley. "Janet Mock Gives The Life ADvice You Need to Hear Right Now." *Refinery29*, December 10, 2014.

Marcotte, Amanda. "Overcompensation Nation: It's time to admit that toxic masculinity drives gun violence." *Salon*, June 13, 2016.

Marech, Rona. "Nuances of gay identities reflected in new language / 'Homosexual' is passé in a 'boi's' life." *SFGate* (blog), February 8, 2004.

Martinez-San Miguel, Yolanda and Sarah Tobias. *Trans Studies: The Challenge to Hetero/Homo Normativities*. New Brunswick: Rutgers University Press, 2016.

Mase III, J. "Islan Nettles' Murder: It Couldn't Have Been Me." *The Huffington Post*, September 5, 2013.

Mauk, Daniel, Perry A and Munoz-Laboy M. "Exploring the Desires and Sexual Culture of Men Who Have Sex with Male-to-Female Transgender Women." *Arch Sex Behav* 42, no. 5 (2013): 793-803.

McDonough, Katie. "Laverne Cox flawlessly shuts down Katie Couric's Invasive questions about transgender people. *Salon*, January 7, 2014.

McKenna, Maddy. "12 Things I've Learned In the First 12 Months With My Vagina." *Kink & Code*, October 3, 2013.

Michael, Joshua. "Bottomed Out." *JoshJenks.com* (blog), February 27, 2016.

———. "Hetero and Homo-normativity Are Everything But 'Normal'." *JoshJenks.com* (blog), June 23, 2015.

Michaels, Samantha. "It's Incredibly Scary to be a Trans Woman of Color Right Now." *Mother Jones,* June 26, 2015.

Mill, John Stuart. *The Subjection of Woman.* Auckland: The Floating Press, 2009.

Milloy, Christin Scarlett. "Beware the Chasers: 'Admirers' Who Harass Trans People." *Slate Magazine,* October 2, 2014.

Mock, Janet. *Redefining Realness: My Path to Womanhood.* New York: Atria Books, 2014.

—. "It Happened to Me: I Told My Boyfriend I Was Born a Boy." *XOJane,* December 7, 2011.

—. "Sharing Our Journey to Marriage with 'Brides' Magazine." *Janet Mock,* November 6, 2015.

—. "How Society Shames Men Dating Trans Women & How This Affects Our Lives." *JanetMock,* September 12, 2013.

Molk, David. *Lion of Siddhas: The Life and Teachings of Padampa Sangye.* Ithaca: Snow Lion, 2008.

Molloy, Parker Marie. "Janet Mock Slams Piers Morgan for Transphobic Questions, Tweets." *Advocate,* February 5, 2014.

—. "California Becomes First State to Ban Gay, Trans 'Panic' Defense." *The Advocate,* September 29, 2014.

Montaigne, Michel de. *Essays.* New York: Penguin, 1958.

Moore, Madison. "On Bottom-Shaming: Is A Bottom Less Of A Man?" *Thought Catalog,* February 19, 2014.

Nadler, Kennedy. "Mira Bellwether and 'Fucking Trans Women. Zine: The Autostraddle Interview." *AutoStraddle,* August 9, 2013.

Nall, Rachel and Ana Gotter. "5 Common Causes of Impotence." *Healthline,* February 3, 2016.

Nardizzi, Vin. *Queer Renaissance Historiography: Backward Gaze.* New York: Routledge, 2009.

Nayfack, Shaikina. "My Dating Life As a Transwoman." *Bust.*

Newbury, Patience. "Curing the Stockholm syndrome of 'stealth'." *Accozzaglia,* July 24, 2013.

Newland, Guy. *Appearance and Reality: The Two Truths in the Four Buddhist Tenet Systems.* Ithaca: Snow Lion, 1999.

Newman, Andy. "City Questions Circumcision Ritual After Baby Dies." *The New York Times,* August 26, 2005.

Nietzsche, Friedrich. *The Gay Science.* Kaufman trans. New York: Vintage, 1974.

—. *The Genealogy of Morals.* Translated by Walter Kaufman. New York: Vintage, 1989.

—. *Thus Spoke Zarathustra.* Graham Parkes trans. Oxford: Oxford University Press, 2009.

O'Connell, Zoe. "Court of Appeals confirms: Stealth trans people having sex are criminals." *Complicity,* June 3, 2013.

Onfray, Michel. *A Hedonist Manifesto.* New York: Columbia University Press, 2016.

Operario, Don, Burton J, Underhill K and Sevelius J. "Men who have sex with transgender women: challenges to category-based HIV prevention." *Aids Behavior* 12, no.1 (2008): 18-26.

O'Toole, Michelle. "This trans woman has some awesome advice for dating whilst trans." *Pink News*, December 3, 2015.

Padawer, Ruth. "The Humiliating Practice of Sex-Testing Female Athletes." *New York Times*, June 28, 2016.

Patrul Rinpoche. *The Words of My Perfect Teacher*. Boston: Shambhala, 1998.

Patti, Magdalena. "The Sexualization of Transwomen." *CatholicTrans*, November 23, 2013.

Phillips, Tony. "The Tranny Chaser Chaser." *Village Voice*, June 22, 2011.

Pittman, Trav. "Four Years to Live: On Violence Against Trans Women of Color." *Huffington Post*, November 24, 2015.

Popkey, Dan. "More gay men describe sexual encounters with U.S. Sen. Craig." *Idaho Statesman*, December 2, 2007.

Prosser, Jay. *Second Skins: The Body Narratives of Transsexuality*. New York: Columbia University Press, 1998.

—. "Judith Butler: Queer Feminism, Transgender, and the Transubstantiation of Sex." In *The Transgender Studies Reader*, Edited by Susan Stryker and Stephen Whittle. New York: Taylor & Francis, 2006.

Prupis, Nadia. "White House Declares Defense of Marriage Act Unconstitutional." *Truthout Magazine*, September 17, 2016.

QueerUMich.com. Accessed September 27, 2016.

Rand, Erin J. *Reclaiming Queer: Activist and Academic Rhetorics of Resistance*. Tuscaloosa: University of Alabama Press, 2014.

Rawes, Peg. *Space, Geometry and Aesthetics: Through Kant and Towards Deleuze*. New York: Palgrave Macmillan, 2008.

Ray, Reginald. *In the Presence of Masters: Wisdom From 30 Contemporary Tibetan Buddhist Teachers*. Boston: Shambhala, 2004.

Raymond, Janice. *The Transsexual Empire: The Making of the She-Male*. New York: Beacon Press, 1979.

Reback, Cathy J, Kaplan RL, Bettcher TM and Larkins S. "The role of the illusion in the construction of erotic desire: narratives from heterosexual men who have occasional sex with transgender Women." *Culture Health & Sexuality Journal* 18, no. 8 (2016): 951-963.

Reed, Kimberly. *Prodigal Sons*. Documentary. 2008. Missoula: Big Sky Productions. HDCAM, DigiBeta, Blu-ray; color/b&w, stereo/Dolby-E.

Reeve, C.D.V. *Plato on Love: Lysis, Symposium, Phaedrus, Alcibiadeswith Selections from Republic and Laws*. Indianapolis: Hackett, 2006.

Reid, Charley. "My Trans Identity Is Not a Fetish." *The Establishment*, March 31, 2016.

—. "Trial and Error: Dating as a Transgender Woman." *Mamamia*, February 7, 2016.

Richards, Jen. "No Wrong Way." *Jen Richards* (blog).

—. *Her Story* (TV show). Speed of Joy Productions, 2015.

Richardson, Sarah H. *Sex Itself: The Search for Male & Female In the Human Genome.* Chicago: University of Chicago Press, 2013.

Ring, Trudy. "This Year's Michigan Womyn's Music Festival Will Be the Last." *The Advocate*, April 21, 2015.

Rios, Julia. "Reaching into the QUILTBAG: The Evolving World of Queer Speculative Fiction" *Apex Magazine,* March 6, 2012.

Roberts, Monica. "Do You Wish To Be A Trans Leader Or A Trans Pariah?" *Transgriot*, January 25, 2016.

—. "Why Were Y'all 'Scurred' of This Trans Attracted Men Panel?" *Transgriot*, January 27, 2016.

—. "Stealth Doesn't Help the Trans Community." *TransAdvocate*, 2013.

—. "Stealth Was a Mistake." *Feministe,* September 8, 2009.

Rodriguez-Jimenez, Jorge. "Op-ed: It Is Time to End Bottom-Shaming." *Advocate*, October. 31, 2014.

Roediger, David. "Critical Studies of Whiteness, USA: Origins and Arguments." *Theoria* 63, no.4 (2001): 72-98.

Rohrbach, Nate. "This Is What It's Like Dating a Transgender Woman." *She 'Said'*, February 26, 2016.

Roiphe, Katie. "The Philosopher and the Student: Was the sage of Colin McGinn really a clear-cut case of sexual harassment?" *Slate*, October 8, 2013.

Salamon, Gayle. *Assuming a Body: Transgender Rhetorics of Materiality.* New York: Columbia University Press, 2010.

Salomonsen, Jone. *Enchanted Feminism: Ritual, Gender, and Divinity Among the Reclaiming Witches of San Francisco.* New York: Routledge, 2002.

Santos, Eduarda Alice. "Brazil: 604 Transgender murders in 7 Years." *Planet Transgender,* December 31, 2015.

Sartre, Jean-Paul. *Saint Genet: Actor and Martyr.* New York: Pantheon, 1963.

Scheman, Naomi. "Queering the Center by Centering the Queer: Reflections on Transsexuals and Secular Jews." In *Feminists Rethink the Self*, Edited by Diana T. Meyers. Boulder: Westview Press, 1997.

Schmalbach, Alessa. "The Genderqueer Movement, as Seen Through a Transwoman's Eyes." *Bullett*, September 8, 2015.

Schultz, Jackson Wright. *Trans/Portraits: Voices From Transgender Communities.* Hanover: Dartmouth College Press, 2015.

Schwartz, Juliana Britto. "At Least 48 Transgender Women Killed In Brazil In January." *Feministing*, January 3, 2016.

Sciortino, Karley. *Being Sexually Successful- Allegedly NYC Podcast.* Episode 7. July 11, 2016.

Scott-Clary, Madison. "Bisexuality and Binaries Revisited." *drab-makyo,* February 13, 2013.

Scutti, Susan. "Transgender People More LIkely To Develop Depression and Anxiety." *Medical Daily,* June 21, 2013.

Serano, Julia. *Excluded: Making Feminist and Queer Movements More Inclusive.* Berkeley: Seal Press, 2013.

—. *Whipping Girl: A transsexual Woman on Sexism and the Scapegoating of Femininity.* Berkeley: Seal Press, 2007.

—. "The Beauty In Us." *Julia Serano,* June 26, 2009.

—. "Autogynephilia and the Psychological Sexualization of MTF Transgenderism." *Julia Serano,* June 26, 2009.

—. "In Defense of Partners." *Julia Serano,* October 8, 2013.

—. "Bisexuality and Binaries Revisited." *Julia Serano,* November 19, 2012.

—. "Rethinking Sexism: How Trans Women Challenge Feminism." *Alternet,* August 4, 2008.

—. "Cocky." *Living Archives on Eugenics Blog,* January 16, 2009.

Shelley, Brook. "Dating Other Women as a Trans Woman: Some Suggestions." *The Toast,* September 8, 2014.

—. "Everyone But Cis Men": Creating Better Safe Spaces for LGBT People." *The Toast,* April 18, 2016.

Shepherson, Charles. *"The Role of Gender and the Imperative of Sex."* In *The Transgender Studies Reader,* Edited by Susan Stryker and Stephen Whittle. New York: Taylor & Francis, 2006.

Shrage, Laurie J., ed. "Trans Identities and First-Person Authority." In *You've Changed: Sex Reassignment and Personal Identity.* Oxford University Press, 2009.

Siderits, Mark. *Buddhism As Philosophy.* Indianapolis: Hackett, 2007.

Siegel, Daniel. *The Developing Mind: How Relationships and the Brain Interact to Shape Who We Are.* New York: The Guilford Press, 2015.

Silverman, Riley. "Trans Sex, Y'all: On the Oversexualization of Trans Identity." *Harlot,* March 29, 2016.

Smith, Nicholas D. "Plato and Aristotle on the Nature of Women." *Journal of the History of Philosophy* 21, no.4 (1983): 467-478.

Sobieraj-Westfall, Sandra. "Transgender Model Geena Rocero Reveals Why She Shared Her Secret." *People.* August 17, 2014.

Sontag, Susan. *Against Interpretation and Other Essays.* New York: Picador, 2001.

—. *Illness as Metaphor and AIDS and Its Metaphors.* New York: Picador, 2001.

St. James, James. "7 Myths About 'Stealth' Transexuals That Undermine Valid Choices." *Everyday Feminism,* April 9, 2015.

Stafford, Zach. "Transgender homicide rate hits historic high in US, says new report." *The Guardian,* November 13, 2015.

Steele, Lauren. "Chris Mosier on Making History as First Trans Member of Team USA." *Rolling Stone,* August 2, 2016.

Steinmetz, Katy. "Why Transgender People Are Being Murdered at a Historic Rate." *Time,* August 17, 2015.

—. "Laverne Cox Talks to TIME About the Transgender Movement." *Time,* May 29, 2014.

Stone, Sandy. "The Empire Strikes Back: A Posttransexual Manifesto." In *The Transgender Studies Reader.* New York: Routledge, 2006.

Stryker, Susan. "My Words to Victor Frankenstein above the Village of Chamonix." In *The Transgender Studies Reader.* New York: Routledge, 2006.

Stryker, Susan and Stephen Whittle eds. *The Transgender Studies Reader.* New York: Routledge, 2006.

Sycamore, Matt Bernstein. *Nobody Passes: Rejecting the Rules of Gender and Conformity.* Berkeley: Seal Press, 2006.

Sykes, Bryan. *Adam's Curse: A Future Without Men.* New York: Norton, 2005.

Taffet, David. "Creating Drama." *Dallas Voice,* January 29, 2016.

Talusan, Meredith. "The Aftermath Of A U.S. Marine's Conviction In The Death Of A Philippine Trans Woman." *Buzzfeed,* January 3, 2016.

Tannehill, Brynn. "What It's Really Like Dating as a Transgender Woman." *The Bilerico Project,* December 3, 2014.

Taylor, Mark C. *Critical Terms for Religious Studies.* Chicago: University of Chicago Press, 1998.

The Cowherds. *Moonshadows: Conventional Truth in Buddhist Philosophy.* Oxford: Oxford University Press, 2010.

The Savage Lovecast. Season 21, Episode 518. Directed by Dan Savage. September 27, 2016.

Thom, Kai Cheng. "6 Things Every Man Who Dates Trans Women Needs to Know." *Everyday Feminism,* October 7, 2015.

Thomas, Calvin. *Male Matters: Masculinity, Anxiety, and the Male Body on the Line.* Chicago: University of Illinois Press, 1996.

Tompkins, Avery Brooks. "'There's No Chasing Involved': Cis/Trans Relationships, 'Tranny Chasers,' and the Future of a Sex-Positive Trans Politics." *Journal of Homosexuality* 61, no. 5 (2014): 766-780.

—. "Intimate Allies: Identity, Community, and Everyday Activism Among Cisgender People with Transgender Partners." PhD dissertation, Syracuse University, 2011.

Tong, Rosemarie. *Feminist Thought: A More Comprehensive Introduction.* New York: Westview, 2013.

Tourjée, Diana. "The Straight Men Who Have Sex With Trans Women." *Broadly Magazine,* September 17, 2015.

—. "'I Love Trannies': Boxer Yusaf Mack Fights for his Attraction to Trans Women." *Broadly Magazine,* March 23, 2016.

"TransOriented: Resources and Support for Men with an Orientation for Transwomen." Accessed September 22, 2016.

"TransOrientedMen.com." Accessed September 22, 2016.

Trungpa, Chogyam. *Glimpses of Abhidharma.* Boulder: Prajna Press, 1978.

Tsering, Geshe Tashi. *Relative Truth, Ultimate Truth: The Foundation of Buddhist Thought,* (Volume 2). Boston: Wisdom Publications, 2008.

Tsoknyi Rinpoche. *Fearless Simplicity: The Dzogchen Way of Living Freely in a Complex World.* Boudhanath: Rangjung Yeshe Publications, 2003.

Turner, William. *Genealogy of Queer Theory.* Philadelphia: Temple University Press, 2000.

Urban Dictionary, s.v. "transamory." Accessed September 27, 2016.

Van Schaik, Sam. *Approaching the Great Perfection: Simultaneous and Gradual Methods of Dzogchen Practice in the Longchen Nyingtig.* Boston: Wisdom Publications, 2004.

Venter, Craig. *A Life Decoded: My Genome: My Life.* New York: Penguin, 2008.

Vrangalova, Zhana. "The Casual Sex Project."

Warren, Karen J. *Ecofeminist Philosophy.* Lanham: Rowman & Littlefield Publishers, 2000.

Wedemeyer, Christian K. *Making Sense of Tantric Buddhism.* New York: Columbia University Press, 2012.

Weinberg, M. S. and Williams, C. "Men Sexually Interested in Transwomen (MSTW): Gendered Embodiment and the Construction of Sexual Desire." *Journal of Sex Research* 47, no. 4 (2010): 374–383.

Wheeler, Michael. "Martin Heidegger." *The Stanford Encyclopedia of Philosophy*, Edited by Edward N. Zalta (Fall 2015 Edition).

Whittle, Stephen. "Where Did We Go Wrong? : Feminism and Trans Theory—Two Teams on the Same Side?" In *The Transgender Studies Reader*, Edited by Susan Stryker and Stephen Whittle. New York: Taylor & Francis, 2006.

Williams, Cristan. "A Rant ABout MTF 'Stealth'." *TransAdvocate*, 2013.

Williamson, Kevin D. "Bradley Manning Is Not a Woman." *The National Review*, August 23, 2013.

—. "Laverne Cox Is Not a Woman." *The National Review*, May 30, 2014.

Willis, Raquel. "The Transgender Dating Dilemma." *Buzzfeed*, October 7, 2015.

Wittgenstein, Ludwig. *Philosophical Investigations.* West Sussex: John Wiley & Sons, 2009.

Wollstonecraft, Mary. *A Vindication of the Rights of Woman.* Boston: Peter Edes, 1792.

Yancy, George. *Dehumanizing Christians: Cultural Competition in a Multicultural World.* Piscataway: Transaction Publishers, 2013.

Zanin, Andrea. "Two generations of fuck you." *Sex Geek* (blog), February 21, 2008.

Zeilinger, Julie. "Laverne Cox On The Group Even More Stigmatized Than Trans Women". *Identities.Mic,* June 19, 2015.

Žižek, Slavoj. *The Pervert's Guide to Ideology.* Directed by Sophie Fiennes. Zeitgeist Films, 2012.

Zuckerman, Esther. "*Transparent's* Trace Lysette on her personal connection to Shea's journey this season." *AVclub,* September 29, 2016.

CPSIA information can be obtained
at www.ICGtesting.com
Printed in the USA
LVOW11s1759120217
523816LV00001B/1/P